Mississippi Barking

Mississippi Barking

Hurricane Katrina and a Life That Went to the Dogs

For Angela,
I'm so
inspired to hear
about your life.
Love,
Chris

Chris McLaughlin

University Press of Mississippi / Jackson

The University Press of Mississippi is the scholarly publishing agency of
the Mississippi Institutions of Higher Learning: Alcorn State University,
Delta State University, Jackson State University, Mississippi State University,
Mississippi University for Women, Mississippi Valley State University,
University of Mississippi, and University of Southern Mississippi.

www.upress.state.ms.us

The University Press of Mississippi is a member
of the Association of University Presses.

Photographs by Carol Guzy

Some names and identifying details have been changed to protect the privacy of
individuals.

First printing 2021
∞

Library of Congress Control Number: 2021938281

Hardback ISBN 978-1-4968-3598-7
Epub single ISBN 978-1-4968-3599-4
Epub institutional ISBN 978-1-4968-3600-7
PDF single ISBN 978-1-4968- 3601-4
PDF institutional ISBN 978-1-4968-3597-0

British Library Cataloging-in-Publication Data available

To my sister Althea McLaughlin
If you hadn't had gone, I wouldn't have known.

And to my friends who dropped everything and traveled far.
You know who you are.

Contents

Prologue

1/9/2006

Dear Supporters of ARF,

It has been almost five months since the levees broke in New Orleans. Five months since Katrina wiped the slate clean along the Gulf Coast in Mississippi. Five months since the worst natural and animal disaster occurred in our country. During these past months, ARF has been among the hundreds of volunteers who flocked to the Gulf to save the animals of Katrina. We crawled under buildings to pull out a feral dog or a litter of puppies living in the filth. We drove the streets at night, searching out the packs who formed as a means of survival. We carried the wounded, fed the starving, and hoped that more could be done for the animals. We drove them up the east coast. We found them new homes, and we watched them die. We did so much with so little.

It's been over a week now since I returned home. Having some distance from the destruction has paved the way for some reflection. It's amazing what sleep will do for a tired soul. I have hope that somehow, some way we will all learn from the lessons Katrina taught us. We will learn that if we don't care, we can't expect others to. If we don't watch over our four-legged friends, no one will. If we don't strengthen the levees, the levees will break.

Natural disasters will continue to happen. We can all count on that. What we don't need to accept is the indifference we witnessed in the aftermath. Because the truth is, Katrina happened to all of us. It happened in every corner of our country. It happened whether we chose to look or not. I thank you for looking. I thank you for caring about the animals.

They are still out there . . .

When I first went to Mississippi and New Orleans, my life looked much different than it does today. In some ways, I am much stronger for the experience, and in some, I am much more disillusioned. What I've learned is that the building of levees begins at home. Caring about each other begins with us. It took a country of people to care about the Katrina kids. Please keep caring.

In the coming weeks, ARF will be facilitating transports out of the Gulf Coast. We need good homes for the kids. We want you to never forget Waveland or Manuel Williams, who lost his beloved chow, Missy, at the Superdome. Please hold on tight to them, so when the levees break again, they will not get swept away.

Mississippi
Barking

Chapter One

A Distant Storm

October 2005. The I-10 out of Mobile, Alabama, is a straight shot into a setting sun. North of the interstate, there are downed trees; to the south, there are downed cities: Biloxi, Gulfport, Long Beach, Bay St. Louis, Waveland. The miles tick by, dusk comes, and the sky turns from gold to rose to lilac. As Mobile slips from my rearview mirror, the world around me turns black. The only light is oncoming traffic, tractor-trailers, and emergency vehicles making their way east. I'm on a three-lane and the lone vehicle heading west.

It has been two months since the Gulf Coast was decimated by the worst natural disaster ever to hit the United States. I am driving a borrowed SUV loaded with bottled water, canned Starbucks coffee, and Milk-Bone dog biscuits. My destination is an animal shelter, hurricane-damaged and floodwater condemned, yet full to capacity, in Waveland, Mississippi—Ground Zero for a hurricane named Katrina.

Mississippi Route 603 intersects the I-10 just west of Bay St. Louis and runs south toward Waveland and the Gulf of Mexico. Long a destination for beachgoers and fishing enthusiasts, the Gulf is a popular tourist attraction, but on this late October night, there is nothing picturesque about it. My headlights expose fractured light poles protruding from the earth, their white metal like broken bones. Turning south on MS 603, I see the remains of a gas station directly across the road. The metal roofing caved in, and a few gas pumps stand at attention in the mud. Amidst the rubble, they looked like weary, tattered soldiers, barely erect, arms by their sides. A quarter-mile down the road, I see the empty shell of a motel, haunted in the gloom, its windows blown out, and its doors missing.

Further down another gas station lies in a deathbed of twisted metal and broken brick. Tattered flags of torn cloth flapped in the wind, some caught in the branches of uprooted trees that had been flung in all directions. On my left, a dish-washing machine half-buried in the mud, evidence that some-one's kitchen was gone. Beds and bicycles, splintered furniture, and chunks of roof, insulation, and drywall littered the road on both sides. Abandoned cars and trucks embedded in the median strip. Buried to the tops of their wheel wells.

Holy shit.

I had never felt so alone. There wasn't a sign of life in any direction. Two months had passed since Katrina but, in south Mississippi, there were no National Guard, police, or fire trucks. There was no sign of *life*. It was just after 10:00 p.m., and the two-lane to the shelter was deserted. The landscape was drenched in the pitch black. It felt like I was in a dysto-pian movie, the last person alive, the hum of my engine the last sound on earth. It was exciting in an eerie sort of way.

I reached for my cell phone to call Eric Phelps, an employee with an international animal welfare organization, In Defense of Animals. He and his then-wife Christy had been working at the Waveland Animal Shelter on a team dispatched from the Pacific Northwestern United States. Before I left Massachusetts, we had spoken, and he had warned me that I'd have to call him when I got to Waveland. The lack of street signs made it impossible to get my bearings or navigate roads, and the animal shelter was hard to find. He was expecting my call.

"Hey, you made it."

"Yeah, I'm here. It only took me a day and a half. I can't believe how bad it looks around here." I leaned forward, squinting, trying to find something to tell me where I was.

"Yeah, and you should see New Orleans. It's a mess. We got delayed picking up some kittens and won't be back until really late. I'm sorry we're not there to meet you." He sounded tired.

"It's OK. I'm sure there will be plenty for me to do. How do I get to the shelter?"

He stayed on the phone with me. After crossing over what appeared to be I-90, Eric told me to take my first right. The only indications that I was at my first right were the many handwritten signs advertising brush and metal hauling, and something called "home removal." He talked me through the twists and turns of a hurricane-shattered neighborhood. It was slow going—the roads were pocked with craters, their depths difficult to judge in the dark—but eventually I arrived at a large, two-story metal structure that Eric assured me was the Waveland Fire Station. It was the first two-storied building I had seen since exiting the interstate. Its hulking metal structure held up to the storm, but the few windows were covered in a blue tarp, and its large bay doors were closed tight.

Eric told me the shelter was behind the station, so I pulled around back. I approached a small building, an oversized shed. A dim source of light silhouetted a swath of a dusty, dry parking area. The light coming from a dirty bulb exposed and dangling from a white electrical cord in the open doorway of the shack. It cast a dim glow. A chain-link fence that had seen its better days surrounded the building. I pulled in and parked. There was barking from inside. I opened the car door, and the late-night Mississippi humidity surrounded me. Within seconds it felt dense and slick on my skin. I stepped out into it and stretched my cramped legs, noticing that the heat felt surprisingly good after hundreds of miles of air conditioning. Still, I was unnerved by the lack of life. I was only a mile from Waveland's busiest intersection on a Friday night, but there were no parties to attend or baseball games to watch. It was just the dogs and me, 1,600 miles away from home.

The Waveland Animal Shelter was located on an unpaved lot between the fire station and public works building. It faced the Waveland sewage treatment plant. The large parking lot was filled with eight to ten vehicles, and every one appeared to be the same color. In the morning light, that color would be revealed as gray—a thin layer of soot, or ash, a combination of sand and dirt: the residue of floodwaters. That night they just looked sad and broken down.

Eric and his wife, Christy, were in New Orleans. They had self-dispatched from their home state of Virginia and had heard about the Waveland Animal Shelter through In Defense of Animals, which operated a sanctuary in northern Mississippi. IDA had been sending folks to the Gulf Coast since the earliest days after the storm. One of those individuals, Connie Durkee, understood pretty quickly that the animals in the Waveland Animal Shelter were in danger. An employee of In Defense of Animals, Connie had left her home in Washington State to help the animals. We met over late-night phone calls in the earliest days and weeks after the storm.

New Orleans shelters were seriously overcrowded. Eric and Christy wanted to scoop up as many kittens as possible to take back to Virginia. For the next few days, it would just be a shelter full of animals, an occasional visit from the staff, and me. We hadn't yet met, but I had heard about the staff. Since mid-September, I had been managing transports out of Waveland to other parts of the US. When Katrina struck, and the levees failed in New Orleans, many first responders, "self-dispatchers," went there. My sister, Althea, a huge animal lover, had self-dispatched. To raise money to get her there, we created an email list of our friends and asked for donations. We promised we'd keep them apprised of Althea's efforts. When she called one morning to tell me there were 100 volunteers at the Lamar Dixon Fairgrounds in Baton Rouge, the makeshift animal shelter for pulling animals out of the flooded city, and that there were over 6,000 addresses of homes where animals were known to have been abandoned, I knew I had to do something. My email pleading for help was sent and shared so many times that within two hours, my phone started ringing. The first call was from Gerry and Lisa O'Mara of Long Island, New York. They wanted to know what they could do.

Gerry was retired from the New York Fire Department and was a first responder during 9/11. He had left the department and was retired now, but he and his wife loved animals. I told him what to pack and where to go, and within a few days, they had loaded up their RV and were on their way to New Orleans.

My experience in the technology field came in handy, as I had been searching the internet to get any and all news I could about the animal rescue efforts. I heard about vacant schools and supermarket parking lots that had been turned into hastily put together animal shelters. I could tell Gerry and Lisa where they should go, who needed the most help, and what they could bring. Once they hit Alabama, they took the I-10 west to Mississippi. A short detour to the coast to see the Gulf landed them at a makeshift animal shelter in Pass Christian. It was there they heard of Waveland.

Waveland, Mississippi, was Katrina. When the storm bolted straight up the Pearl River, Waveland sat just east of its path—the most destructive side of a hurricane. And by the time Katrina blew herself out, Waveland had lost 85 percent of its buildings. Not "lost," as in misplaced, but destroyed, demolished, obliterated. Imagine your home today and all of your possessions, your photographs, your furniture, keepsakes, clothing, silverware . . .

Your animals . . .

Imagine it all . . .

Then imagine evacuating for a monster storm, and when weeks later, you are finally allowed to return you can't find one photograph, not one thing that resembles anything, not even a comb . . . your comb. Never mind your bathroom, or your porch, your kitchen or your bed . . . you no longer own a comb.

The animal shelter sat one mile from the coast and was completely flooded. Those people who did not evacuate clung to their roofs and sought higher ground in two-story buildings and the I-10 overpass, six miles inland. It's still not known how many people perished as a result of Katrina.

The storm brought rescuers from all over the country, but only a few outside of the In Defense of Animals staff had stumbled on Waveland. Connie had been given my number by Gerry, and during late-night calls, she'd tell me about the rumors she had heard and the glaring glances the staff cast at the first responders. The Waveland Animal Shelter was something straight out of the movie *Friday the 13th*. Connie believed that the staff didn't care about the animals and resented their positions at the shelter. She refused to leave the shelter out of fear the animals would come to harm in her absence. She asked if there was any way I could figure out how to get the animals out of there. We came to understand the staff would have preferred to put all of them down if we didn't.

A Quonset hut had been set up outside for the first responders, and Connie, Eric, and Christy slept inside at night. They took turns ensuring someone was always onsite to protect the animals. By late October, Connie had returned home to Washington State. I knew I would be the only one there that first night given the delays in New Orleans. I pushed on the chain-link gate, and it opened, the metal scraping along the gash it had carved in the concrete floor. The dogs quieted, but I could hear their restless movements as they waited in tense expectation.

Looking up, I saw the caved-in roof, a gaping hole, and the night sky beyond. The first corridor of kennels was entirely exposed to the elements, though thankfully, the cages were empty. I took a right into a large entryway where a commercial-sized, stainless steel tub lined one wall. The tub was filled with dirty dishes and bowls. Flies buzzed around my head, and I could feel the crunch of stale kibble under my feet. The place smelled of wet dog, bleach, and feces.

I approached the first cages. The first dog I saw was a reddish-golden Collie type with a long, pointed nose. She approached the door to greet me, and I squeezed my fingers through the small, rusty, diamond-shaped links. Her wet nose sniffed the air and brushed my fingers. I looked down the row of cages. The light was dim, but I could make out the small paws and noses that strained to push their way under the gates and through the spaces in the wire. I continued down the row. Some of the dogs were eager for my attention and waddled up to me, tails wagging, their small yips bouncing from the walls. Many of them cowered in the corner. I continued on, peering into each cage. Many looked scared and lonely. At that moment, they looked like me.

One dog, an Australian Shepard, huddled in the farthest corner of her cell and shook violently when I approached her kennel. I crouched, trying to make myself look small, and talked to her in the kindest, softest voice I could muster. "Come here, baby, it's OK." She wouldn't move. I opened the door to her cage, knelt on the sticky floor, and held out my hand. She sniffed the air briefly, and her body shifted slightly. I reached to touch her matted coat. She hesitated, seemed to consider the possibility, and then turned her head away. She wanted no part of me.

I leaned against the cool concrete of her cell. The place reeked of urine and feces, with a touch of something old and damp, like mold. The little Aussie eyed me suspiciously and pushed herself further into the corner of her cage. I laid my head back and closed my eyes.

What the hell was I doing here?

After a moment or two, I looked around and up, and I saw it for the first time: a black-and-gray spotted line, about a foot in width, hemming every wall. It was the high-water mark. Katrina's storm surge crested at twenty-eight feet in Waveland. Once receded, the city sat in five feet of dead, polluted water. The shelter and its abandoned animals simmered in the muck, in the late summer heat, for days.

I looked at my little cellmate and again offered her my hand. She started toward me and then thought better of it. When I got up to leave, I could feel her eyes watching me.

I went back outside to consider my options. My eyes adjusted to the darkness that surrounded me. Kicking up small puffs of dust as I walked, I went to the back of the SUV and reached into my cooler for a can of Starbucks coffee. The ice I'd purchased in Mobile had not yet melted and thankfully it was still ice-cold; it was going to be a long night. A big box of Milk-Bones was packed in the back next to the first aid kit I had picked up at a Costco back in Connecticut. I opened the box and grabbed a handful of biscuits. I walked back into the shelter.

That first night there were twenty dogs and seventeen cats in the Waveland Animal Shelter. They all needed their cages cleaned. Feces and urine pooled on the floor of every kennel: puppies played and tumbled in it, and older dogs had no choice but to pace back and forth in the mess. Some of them were simply lying on the dirty concrete floor, listless and despondent. There were water dishes—large, galvanized steel pails—but they were dented and rusty, and most were completely dry. For how long I couldn't tell, but it was still hot as hell in Mississippi.

There were signs of neglect in most of the cages, and it grieved my heart. The food bowls were rusted and empty. The animals' little noses were crusty, their fur matted, and some had tear-stained faces, small creeks running downstream from their eyes. There was no bedding or toys, and the open drainpipe that ran along the back of each cage was filled with dried feces and puddles of a putrid liquid. Flies were crawling on the heads of puppies, and some of the kittens were so young their eyes weren't even open. Some were curled up in little balls with their moms, but many were on their own. The ones with mothers and littermates seemed to be faring the best. Their little meows broke my heart, and I pulled them from the small metal cages that lined the wall of a back room and held them to my chest. I'd tend to them first.

The cat room was in the back, a small space that emitted a powerful ammonia-type odor. The bowls were filthy and had not been cleaned, probably not since Eric and Christy had left for New Orleans a few days before my arrival. It looked like it too. Litter boxes were filled with crusted feces and clumps of urine. The water bowls were nearly empty and had bits of disintegrated litter and swollen bits of kibble in them. The kittens cried out to me when I looked into their little stainless-steel cages, and the momma cats paced, as if not knowing what next to do.

The commercial-sized sink in the entryway only drew cold water, but I washed the puppies as well as I could. I wiped the cages down with a threadbare towel and some cleaning supplies I found on a counter in the entryway. Most of the puppies held onto my arms for dear life when I lifted them up from the concrete floor, their little paws wrapped around my forearm as if pleading for me not to let go. Some of them whimpered like the babies they were. I held them to my chest and told them they were going to be alright.

There was a box in the entryway, overflowing with leashes and leads. I assumed that they had been donated, but it was unlikely that they had ever been used because they all still had tags. I grabbed a few leashes and collars and made my way back to the cages. The larger dogs I walked, but because of the total darkness, we didn't venture far.

It was 1:00 a.m. when my work completed. I took one last look at the animals. I knew that some of them were going to need medical attention, but I couldn't do any more that night. Eric had told me I could bunk in the Quonset hut, but when I opened the door, I couldn't see a damn thing, and the vast darkness scared me. I opted for the back of the SUV. It would be hot, but I'd be safe. I lay on top of my sleeping bag and tried to slow my racing mind. I didn't know what tomorrow would bring, but I found myself eagerly anticipating Eric and Christy's arrival. I had never worked in an animal shelter or been exposed to the epic destruction of a natural disaster. Exhausted, I couldn't sleep, anticipating the rising sun.

When I turned forty my mom gifted me a session with an astrologer. The cassette tape of that session is long gone, but I remember very clearly that she mentioned I was reaching a point in my life where I was questioning my contribution to the world. That as I entered my forties, I would reflect back on my life and yearn for something more meaningful. That this quest would require travel, but after spending my late twenties and early thirties in an airplane for my high-tech career, I was perfectly happy at home in Massachusetts and had little desire to travel anywhere, anymore.

Yet here I was, forty-six years old, single and unemployed, lying in the back of an SUV, in a parking lot littered with stranded vehicles, 1,600 miles from home. My heart full, my fear subsided, I felt emboldened by a newfound strength. Two days prior, I got in the SUV and headed south. Alone. Destination? A flooded shelter in a coastal town I had never heard of before. I'd been online for a month trying to help the first responders and my sister get information, supplies, or more volunteers. Now I was here.

My thoughts drifted to the last five years. I had been mostly unemployed after walking away from a very stressful six-figure executive position for a large Boston investment company;

my status as the first woman executive in the department was a handicap I couldn't overcome. A team of twenty-six individuals in my organization, a yearly bonus guaranteed. That was late August 2001, two weeks before 9/11, and I had no idea I'd be out of work for the majority of the next six years or that 9/11 would not only destroy lives and buildings but careers. A return to college to achieve a lifetime goal of gaining a bachelor's degree offered some sense of accomplishment, but my life had mainly felt insignificant during that time. As I drifted off to sleep, I imagined I had found something I could do and make right, something worth living for. Something profoundly meaningful.

Morning broke with bright sun and a warm breeze. I rolled off my sleeping bag and took a look outside. The world had lost all color. It was as if I were in the middle of a black-and-white photograph. A landscape of sepia-colored tones surrounded me. Everywhere and everything was a dull brownish-gray.

I climbed outside to take a closer look around. The dirt parking lot was filled with fire department vehicles, vans, trucks, and a few SUVs. Katrina had entombed every one. There were piles of debris in a small field next door, but a closer look revealed waterlogged firefighting gear, left to rot in the hot sun. Filing cabinets, their drawers hanging open, spit pieces of paper, shriveled and pocked, their corners brown. Parked next to the fire station, shielded from the sun, was a bright, shiny, red ladder truck with either North Carolina or Wisconsin stenciled on the doors, I can't remember which. Later that day, I watched the Waveland firefighters polish her like a trophy they had won in a competition and never wanted to forget. In a scene that was bathed in brushstrokes of brown and gray, that truck was the only exception.

I walked back to the SUV. The bright sun rose in a cloudless sky. The air was warming fast. I climbed into the driver's seat as quietly as possible. It had only been a few hours since the animals had fallen asleep, and I didn't want to wake them. It was 7:00 a.m. when I turned the key in the ignition and headed a mile south to the Gulf of Mexico.

Within a few blocks, I saw the vast and sparkling blue of the water. Nothing was obstructing my view because everything— trees and homes—were gone. Gulfside Street ends at the Gulf, and I idled there for a moment, admiring the beautiful sunrise to the southeast. But to the north, inland, it was a no-man's land, stretching as far as I could see. Trees had been snapped in two, their jagged edges jutting like giant spears from the earth. The ground was littered with metal, paper, brick, and concrete. It looked like a nuclear bomb went off in the middle of Waveland—like something catastrophic had happened there, like a place where people once lived.

Just a few months earlier, Waveland's waterfront had been a quiet and idyllic seaside destination for the affluent from New Orleans. The white sand beaches drew vacationers from all parts, and historical buildings, casinos, and other tourist attractions had lined the coast from Waveland to Biloxi. Antebellum houses with stately porches overlooked lush green lawns that faced south to the crystal blue Gulf of Mexico. Centuries-old oaks grew in their extravagant, meandering habits, with great, groaning limbs that stretched out wide and ran parallel to the ground before arching toward the sky. They would have been in full leaf in late August, the pending hues of autumn not yet coloring their leaves. Waveland, before Katrina, was just a sleepy, coastal Mississippi town.

But by late October, everything from the shores of the Gulf north to the train tracks six blocks inland was in ruins. Flood-proof stilts, some as high as twenty feet, remained standing, but the homes they were meant to protect were gone. Concrete staircases led to nowhere. The trees that were still standing were leafless skeletons, their bark peeling or stripped away, and boats had been tossed into the middle of residential roads. In one neighborhood, a car rested upright on its front bumper, its rear axle leaning against what was left of a large tree. The tree's brawny trunk was snapped in two like a matchstick. The car appeared suspended in the air like it had been hung for evil deeds. The world had been turned upside down.

South Beach Boulevard parallels the Mississippi coastline from the town of Lakeshore on the Louisiana border to the I-90 Bridge at Bay St. Louis. A one-lane road running east to west, Katrina chewed it up and spat it out. Yellow police tape draped on jersey barriers warned me of the large, gaping craters up ahead. I turned and traveled the westbound lane. On my left, the Gulf of Mexico looked picture-perfect. The sky had begun to sear a hazy white blue with the first hues of a day that promised to be hot. Not a cloud was in the sky. A soft, gentle breeze kicked up small waves that licked at the shore.

Further down the road, concrete posts jutted from the water in a straight line, like soldiers marching out to sea, but the boardwalk they supported had washed away. For miles and miles, the beach was covered with debris, both manmade and natural. I turned north. Every street looked identical to the last. None had names—their signs were gone. I drove slowly, keeping my eyes on the road, and I didn't linger for long out of respect for the few people I came across. The few I saw were burly white men with construction hats and reflective vests. One block inland, at the beginning of one street, an American flag hung from the broken limb of the remainder of a giant oak tree. On both sides of the street, I could see driveways that led to concrete slabs, the only evidence of where homes once stood. I turned right and then another quick right, and headed back to the waterfront. Looking east along the shoreline, I could see a roof and the top floors of a building peeking from the waters. After a few blocks, I turned left and headed inland again.

The silence is what I most remember of that first drive along the coastline of Waveland. Despite the destruction, the gentle beauty of the Gulf endured: soft waves gently lapped a debris-strewn shore, and a lone migratory bird perched on a splintered mooring. The sun peeked over the horizon and winked in soft yellows while uprooted trees slumbered hundreds of yards off-shore, their trunks rocking in the gentle waters of the Gulf, their branches breaking the horizon like hands reaching from the sea. The gulf coast had become a burial ground. The temperature was already in the low 90s at 7:30 a.m., and the day promised to be a late summer dream, but the beaches here would have no sunbathers today. The light breeze off the water had no leaves to rustle. The birds did not sing.

I turned around to head back to the shelter. I knew that the animals would be waking, and I wanted someone to be there when they did. I passed a police car and a road crew; both eyed me suspiciously. I was a single female, sporting expensive sunglasses and driving a large SUV with a Massachusetts tag. There probably hadn't been many of us around lately.

Crossing over Highway 603, I saw a large Walmart sign still standing on its metal posts, but pockmarked with large holes from flying debris and missing most of its letters. A few cars were turning into the parking lot. Aside from the police, they were the only cars on the road. I longed to see other people, so I turned into the Walmart lot. A makeshift sign hung in front of a large white tent announcing: "We're open!" People were filing in and out. Seeing all those people made me feel a little bit less alone.

The tent was packed with folks, but it was eerily quiet. There were no display racks or shelving. Instead, rows and rows of long banquet tables were piled high with personal care and food items, and cases of bottled water were stacked along the insides of the tent walls. Potato chips and other food items that did not require refrigeration were plentiful. There was, critically, no coffee. Most of the people who filed in had a glazed and tired look about them—their eyes downcast, their movements slow. Occasionally folks would recognize a neighbor or friend, and a subdued reunion would follow. Tears flowed. Faces turned away. Some couples murmured between themselves as they discussed their purchases, and the cashiers and staff were cheerful as they went about their jobs. The forced joyfulness in their voices held a surreal tone. And despite their noble efforts to be lighthearted and to brighten up the place, the feeling in the air was heavy.

I searched the aisles more out of curiosity than necessity. I made a note of what was there in case I needed something I'd forgotten to bring. I paid for my warm bottle of water and exited the tent into a bright and glorious day.

Not knowing if the staff would show up, I headed back to the shelter. As I passed the fire department, there were a few people outside. I pulled over and got out. Nine hours earlier, it had felt as if I was the only soul for miles, but now that the sun was shining, the truck bay doors were open and a small card table was set up inside. A guy in a blue short-sleeved shirt that read "Waveland Fire Department" sat at the table. I hadn't spoken a word to anyone since the phone call to Eric the night before, and I was lonely, hot, and tired. I wanted a friend. I introduced myself: he was short and muscular with a warm, easy smile, and when I told him I was there to help the animals, he held out his hand and told me his name was Tony. His handshake was soft yet firm. I liked him immediately. He walked me around and showed me the small bathroom on the first floor. There was a shower stall with a clean white liner that looked to have been thrown up in a hurry. "It's not much," he said, "but it's yours to use whenever you need."

Tony walked me through a large, open area that served as both kitchen and cafeteria. Long tables were stacked with boxes of donated supplies. More boxes lined the walls, filled with toothpaste, deodorant, toothbrushes and combs, bottles of aspirin and Band-Aids, granola bars, and soda. I waved to a few firemen who sat casually talking at some tables in the middle of the room as Tony shouted out, "This is Chris from Boston, and she's here to help the shelter!" The guys smiled, and one yelled, "Welcome!" Tony walked me back outside and showed me another Quonset hut where they slept at night, then told me if I needed anything, anything at all, I should feel free to knock on the door. "It doesn't matter what time it is," he said.

Tony and I became fast friends, and I felt safer knowing he was there. The Waveland firefighters had suffered their own losses. Their city was in shambles, and their trucks were destroyed, but every time I saw them, they smiled easily and made me feel like one of their own.

Next to the fireman's Quonset hut was a large, open flapped green tent. Tony explained that donations had been coming in nonstop from all over the country. There were heaps of clothing. A long table was stacked with used books, and there were piles of shoes, shirts, and children's toys. Even though it was early

in the morning on a Saturday, a few people solemnly picked
through the piles. They went about their business silently, their
shoulders slumped.

When I pulled up to the shelter, another car was out front.
The dogs were barking, and I heard banging from inside. In the
entryway was a young man, mid-to-late twenties, his dark hair
unkempt, and his shirt loose, wet with sweat, hung over baggie
pants. He seemed as surprised as I was to see another person. I
introduced myself and offered my hand. He told me his name
was Larry, and he was glad to have some help. He said he didn't
expect any of the other staff to come in that day.

During the visit at the fire department, I mentioned I was worried I didn't have enough help to take care of the animals. Tony
told me FEMA was down the road and might be able to help.
When I told him I was going to try to round up some folks, he
let me borrow one of the Waveland FD pickup trucks. "Come
right back," he said. "I don't want the chief to see you out riding
around in it. I'd get in a lot of trouble if he did."

I quickly learned how naïve I was to think FEMA would
help with the animals. I followed Tony's directions and turned
into a large parking lot that had a steady stream of vehicles
entering and exiting. I followed signs to the main entrance
and waited in line for one of the tables staffed with an official-
looking person in a light blue shirt to become available. Within
twenty minutes, a middle-aged man motioned me to his table. I
told him I was working at the animal shelter, and I needed help
with the animals. He looked up at me with a quizzical look on
his face as if I'd spoken in a foreign language. "Try REMA," he
said. "Next door."

REMA? What the hell was REMA? He busied himself with the papers in front of him, making it clear to me we were done. I walked away. When I got to the parking lot, I asked another man in a FEMA shirt where I could find REMA. He pointed to the large parking lot next door.

The Rainbow Emergency Management Agency, or "REMA," had descended on Waveland after the storm. A bunch of good-hearted hippies, straight out of the 1960s and mostly from North Carolina, had ironically joined forces with some local and out-of-state church groups. Together they offered a much better coordinated and accessible alternative to FEMA. Their large encampment was right down the road from Walmart. Operating a food kitchen in a large enclosed tent, known to all as the New Waveland Café, they served up healthy food, live music, and entertainment. Right next door to their large gathering of tents and RVs was the building housing the Federal Emergency Management Agency. And while FEMA had the fancy, brick-and-mortar building, with official-looking government vehicles of every shape and size, REMA was the outfit providing food, solace, and rest to the homeless of Hancock County.

Small tents surrounded the much larger tent that was the center of activity. Many people were milling about. Conversation and laughter everywhere. Their large flaps pulled back; each tent was like its own little store. Some had tables of clothing while others had tools, kitchenware and utensils, books, and small pieces of furniture—the things one might need to rebuild a life. One tent was staffed with medical personnel.

I walked among them, fascinated by what I saw. Most of the men sported beards and had colored handkerchiefs holding back long hair while the women wore loose and brightly colored clothing. I felt like I had been transported to a Grateful Dead tailgating party. I could hear music coming from the large tent, and I walked inside.

A very tall man, in brightly colored clothing, long Rasta hair, and a large toothy smile greeted me at the opening. "Welcome!" he announced. "Food's over there!" I told him I was working at the animal shelter down the road, and I needed some folks to help me out. "Heather! You need Heather!" he exclaimed. "Follow me."

We went back out to the smaller tents, and at each one, he asked if anyone had seen Heather. We found her in one of the tents furthest away from the center of activity. Heather was a thirty-something redhead who burst into a grin and a hug when I was introduced as "Chris, who is volunteering at the animal shelter." "What do you need?" she asked. "I could use some animal-lovers if you have them!" was all I could think to say.

Within twenty minutes, Heather had rounded up seven other REMA folks who couldn't wait to spend time with some animals. They piled into the bed of the fire department pickup, and we headed back to the shelter. When we arrived at the fire department, Tony and a few of the guys were standing out front. Tony gave me a sheepish look, and his eyes darted to an official-looking man with white hair and a big belly; his shirt read "CHIEF" in bright red letters. I knew we'd been busted. I smiled broadly as the REMA folks piled out of the back and cab. I walked up to the chief with my best smile and put out my hand. "Chief, I can't thank you guys enough for helping me get some folks back here to help us at the shelter." He reluctantly shook my hand and looked at Tony. The chief was not amused.

Those folks made my day. While some held or walked the animals, others started cleaning the shelter. I had learned very quickly that running an animal shelter didn't require an education. All one needed was a caring and eager heart. Throw in some common sense and a willingness to get dirty, and the foundation has been built.

Every one of my newfound friends was so loving and gentle as they placed the new leads around the dog's necks and gently led them outside. It was hot and humid, so the walks were brief. Patches of shade were found where the dogs could be tethered and exposed to fresh air and clean water. Worried about the Australian Shepard from the night before, I brought Heather over to meet her. I left them alone so I could start cleaning the cages and kennels with the others. Later that morning, my heart galloped in my chest as I watched Heather skipping through the parking lot with the scared dog hesitantly trotting on the other end of the lead.

The REMA folks spent three hours with me that day. By the time they left, it felt like a much happier and more caring place. The towels were folded and stacked neatly, and the collars and leads hung from nails for easy access. All the bowls were clean and filled, and the puppies no longer smelled of their poop. Having spent some time outside, they now lay peacefully in their cages, new beds made of blankets and sheets. I relaxed a bit outside by the backdoor, my mind racing through the events of the day. I laid my head back against the wall. The brief moment of quiet was a welcomed friend. The animals in the shelter, which I now felt were my sole responsibility, were still in varying stages of distress. Some had open wounds and runny noses. The puppies and kittens were inconsolable and, when not sleeping, made desperate little sounds. Many of them were scared. Only time and care could fix that.

Eric had left me the phone number to a local veterinarian who was driving the coast and helping the shelters destroyed by the storm. Her name was Jacquie Broome. That first full day in

Waveland, I called Dr. Broome four times and left messages. At 4:00 p.m., my phone rang. A strong female voice with a deep Mississippi drawl asked me what I needed. I didn't know what I needed. I told her I was most concerned about a white pit bull I had named "Petey." The leather collar and chain someone had put around his neck had become embedded in his skin while he outgrew its original size, and the area was so infected I was hesitant to remove the chain and clean the wound myself. His body was bright pink, and his skin, the color of cotton candy. His hair was thin or missing. He lay still in his cage. Petey was so listless, and his wound so gruesome, that I knew he needed medical attention the most. He was the first pit bull I had ever met. Like most, I had been led to believe they were a vicious breed, but there was nothing mean about him. He lay so still in his cage, his eyes following me when I walked by. I made up my mind then and there that I was going to save him.

The little Aussie Shepard, despite her brief romp with Heather, showed little improvement, and no amount of kind words could get her out of the farthest corner of her cage. She shook violently anytime I went near her. In between the cleaning of the other cages, I would slowly approach and gently open the door to her cage. She would take a hesitant step toward my out-stretched hand and then quickly retreat. I wanted to take her for a walk. I wanted to prove to her that not all people were cruel.

I begged Jacquie Broome to come.

Jacquie Broome, DVM, ran a veterinary hospital on wheels and dispensed care out of her pickup truck along the Gulf Coast. Even though Katrina had slammed into her farm and washed away her Gulfport veterinary practice, she was doing all she could. Many of her own animals did not survive the hurricane, but her home was livable.

Dusk was settling on my first full day on the Gulf Coast when I heard a car engine out front. A large white van pulled up. The driver stopped, the passenger door opened, and a large woman wearing a baseball cap, jeans, and a badly stained T-shirt climbed out. She looked strong, with thick, broad shoulders, and her dark brown hair was pulled back in a long ponytail.

"Girl, how in the *hell* did you find yourself in this place? You are in *the* worst shelter in this state, if not the country."

I smiled, approached, and extended my hand. The side door of the van sprung open, and twelve young, mostly female, veterinary students spilled out of the vehicle. They hovered around the doc and waited for instructions. Jacquie asked me what they could do. I had labored over the animals since the REMA folks left, and the extra hands almost brought tears to my eyes. Larry, the one shelter worker who showed up for work that day, preferred sitting and not working up too much of a sweat, so unless specifically asked, he did nothing.

"The kittens are out back and could really use some attention," I told the vet students. "If some of you could clean their litter boxes, give them fresh water and food, that would be great!"

I asked the others if they could walk some of the larger dogs, and explained that the puppies needed constant cleaning and affection. I told Jacquie about Petey. She agreed that he had to be seen immediately. A quick order to the students sent them into action, and within minutes the shelter was alive with busybodies, all of them knowledgeable, all of them competent. Some set to walking dogs; others cleaned cages and filled water bowls. "Follow me," I said to Jacquie as we walked down the row of cages.

Petey's eyes barely acknowledged us when we approached. I had put a worn blanket under him to offer him some comfort from the hard, stained, concrete floor, but the leather collar and chain that had become a part of his neck and the skin condition that covered his body was causing him significant discomfort. Jacquie Broome knelt down and extended her hand. Petey didn't respond, but I sensed he was not afraid. I felt his hope. Within minutes she had gently peeled the pus-encrusted collar from his neck, the leather so decrepit that it came away in bits and pieces. The metal ringlets of the chain came off easier. After directing a student to retrieve supplies from the van, she started cleaning his wound. With gentle strokes, Dr. Broome gingerly washed away small pieces of leather and skin. Underneath, his neck was raw and bloody, but Petey lay there patiently while she worked. I whispered words of comfort to our little charge and watched as Jacquie shook her head in disgust.

"This collar has been around his neck for a very long time," she said.

"He's probably had it on since he was a puppy."

I cast my head down and looked into his vulnerable eyes.

"It's OK, boy," I said. "It's OK, now."

When she was finished, she handed me a small tube of antibiotic ointment and instructed me on how to apply it. "Three times a day," she said. "And make sure the wound stays real clean, or he'll be prone to infection."

Their visit lasted an hour. By the time they all climbed back into the van, I was loaded up with instructions and good feelings. I was assured none of the animals had anything life-threatening, and I had enough medication to take care of most of the infections. Dr. Broome had given me what she could, but she couldn't give me everything I would need: she had to visit another shelter that night. Dr. Broome thanked me and left me with a word of caution: the Waveland Animal Shelter was not where you wanted to end up if you were an animal needing a kind hand or a safe place. The shelter had earned a reputation for being indifferent to the welfare of animals; mostly uninterested in placing animals in loving homes, they killed many more than they saved. Rumors had circulated for years that purebred dogs were sold out the back door to friends and the occasional county official. Stories that the animal control officers, Chase and Chubby, bred pit bulls and engaged in dogfighting were not the imagination of a few overzealous rescuers. Jacquie asked if I would be willing to document what I saw. If I'd ask the others that came to do the same. I told her I would. "I want this place shut down," she said. "Be careful." Then she was gone.

After Dr. Broome left, Larry and me sat outside. A gentle breeze offered little relief from the heat. The sun still burned hot and hazy in the sky, a glowing orb of color. In a moment of kindness, he told me he didn't want to leave me there alone. We talked for an hour, and he told me about the shelter. How the unwanted puppies and kittens were a constant stream from neglectful owners. How abuse cases were rampant, and it was common for an older dog to be surrendered only to be replaced by a new puppy. Spay and neuter was unaffordable or against the religion of some. Adoption rates were low in the best of times.

He told me that many days he'd had to put down as many as fifty dogs. He told me things I wanted to instantly forget. When the sun had set, and Larry had left, I pulled out my laptop and sent another Animal Rescue Front report—the daily emails I had been sending to friends and family since September. They were my only link to the world I had left behind, a world where most animals were safe, cherished, and loved. Where they were almost exclusively "indoor dogs" and not tethered outside to a chain. Where they were members of the family and not a means to intimidate visitors to one's property. And where they were almost always neutered. I talked about the small victories that day: Petey getting much-needed care, and the terrified Aussie Shepard, allowing Heather to take her for a walk through the parking lot. The animals did seem a bit calmer now. After shutting my laptop down, I took one last walk through the shelter. They were sleeping comfortably in their cages, and the kittens purred in their mothers' fur. I walked slowly and checked every single one. They were mine now. I pulled the string on the naked bulb in the entryway and watched the world go dark. With one more look at the star-filled night sky, I crawled into the back of the SUV and tried to sleep.

I didn't know what tomorrow would bring. Would it be the day I'd meet the director, Roberta? The stories Connie and Eric told me didn't paint a kind picture of her and frankly scared the shit out of me. Eric and Christy were going to stop in Waveland on their way through to Virginia the next day, and I looked forward to meeting them in person for the first time; however, once they were gone, I knew I'd be alone with the staff. The chances of another rescuer stumbling upon Waveland weren't good as most of the folks were self-dispatching to New Orleans. New Orleans was the story that garnered the most attention from the beginning, while Mississippi was treated as an afterthought, a mere byproduct of the hurricane—when, in fact, Mississippi *was* the main event.

In Defense of Animals had been to the coast many times since August, but they were overwhelmed with the need. I was pretty certain I was on my own, and I didn't want to trouble the firefighters with my concerns. I was reluctant to be seen as negative or judgmental in any way.

On Sunday morning, my second full day on the coast, I dragged myself out of my sleeping bag and headed to the fire station for a quick shower. When I got back to the shelter, I heard voices in the back room. I figured now was as good a time as any to meet the other staff. I could hear chatter about their days off, and when I walked into the room, I saw two women sitting at a small table. I introduced myself and extended my hand. I made a self-deprecating comment about being the first "Yankee" they'd probably ever met, but it didn't go over too well. Neither of them was amused, and their welcome to me was chilly at best. Their names were Roberta and Tori. Both white with stern faces, Roberta had a long dark ponytail pulled back from her face, while Tori, short in stature, had long blond hair worn freely. Roberta introduced herself as the shelter manager. Neither accepted my extended hand.

Larry and another man who I assumed to be Chase, sauntered in and dropped into chairs. The conversation between Larry and I from the night before had been, apparently, on the down-low. The camaraderie he and I shared was gone. He didn't look my way.

And the kennels were a mess.

No one had done a thing.

It wasn't until Chase got up and headed out to the kennels that anything started to happen. I followed. He grabbed a long hose and started hosing down the insides of the kennels while the animals were still in them. I asked him to please stop so I could get the animals out before they got soaked with the cold water. I started moving the larger dogs outside and tethered them in shady spots. I didn't want them to get sprayed with urine and feces. I started bathing the puppies in the large sink. The water was cool, so I worked quickly. After I dried them as best I could I placed them back in a clean kennel with fresh towels, blankets, and water. When Chase was finished hosing down the kennels, they could be fed.

Eric and Christy arrived late that morning with fourteen cats and kittens from New Orleans. They were running behind schedule, so the visit was brief. Eric and I walked out back so I could tell him about Dr. Broome's visit and give him an update on Petey's neck wound. Eric happily helped me apply another round of antibiotic ointment to the wound. A weeks-old puppy had been surrendered to me that morning, and I had wrapped him in a blanket and held him to my chest. I wanted him to feel my body heat and hear my heartbeat. I don't know how I knew this was what had to be done, but I trusted my instincts. Fortunately, I had found a small plastic bottle feeder and some powdered puppy formula. I kept the bottle filled and with me all morning. Frequently I held it to his little mouth. He took it easily. When Christy and Eric left, they took him with them. Christy could hold him on the trip back to Virginia, and he'd get better care and more attention from them. I was happy to know he would be leaving Waveland forever.

The only open restaurant in town was Sonic, and while, generally, I'm not too fond of fast food, an aversion to starvation and an opportunity to bond encouraged me to place an order when the staff congregated for lunch. And hard as I tried, I was unable to engage any of them in any lasting conversation.

I learned how to run a shelter by following my instincts. The staff looked at me like I was nuts, but I didn't care. As the time for me to leave became closer, I pulled Larry aside to show him how to care for Petey's wound and administer the eye drops for the kittens with infections. He seemed my best chance at it getting done. At one point, he looked at me and shook his head in acknowledgment, and while I wanted so badly to believe he would follow through, I didn't really hold out much hope. But the time had come for me to head to what I thought was my final destination. New Orleans was littered with stray dogs, and puppies were being born under deserted buildings. I was needed there. And the transports I had started from Cape Cod had to continue.

For two and a half days, I immersed myself in caring for the Waveland animals. The work was exhausting, dirty, and heart-breaking, but the animals were the reason I came, and they were going to get the best possible care while I was there. While Roberta and Tori hovered deep in thought over a jigsaw puzzle, Larry, Chase, and I sprayed down the kennels. When I witnessed it happening with puppies inside, I continued to question it. Larry gave a lame excuse of having nowhere to put them, but you didn't need a veterinary degree to know that showering a feces-filled kennel with an animal in it, much less vulnerable puppies, was just plain stupid and dangerous. I implored them to not do it anymore. Luckily Larry was impressionable, and he started to follow my lead. Chase eventually did too. Roberta and Tori rarely ventured out to the kennels, preferring to stay out back in the office, gossiping and smoking cigarettes.

When Monday came, it was time for me to pack up and head to New Orleans. I had networked with some of the animal rescue groups in the New Orleans area for the two months before my arriving on the coast, and I was really looking forward to having the company of people who didn't think I'd blown a gasket. Ever since watching the movie *The Big Easy* in 1986, I had longed to visit New Orleans, and I devoured all I could about the city. Between reading every James Lee Burke novel and ordering some Cajun music online, I had a connection to the city that was visceral and inexplicable. I couldn't wait to get there.

Roberta's demeanor towards me was a bit more pleasant that morning. I told her I was leaving to go to New Orleans, and she wished me luck. No doubt, she was eager to be rid of me. I grabbed a brand-new collar out of the large box of collars and leads, and I went to the kennel that held the golden collie mix. Every chance I had the past two days, I spent time with "Honey," a name that came naturally given the honey-hued color of her coat and her sweet personality. I opened the gate to her cage, and she slowly walked out, her head lowered. I gently placed the collar around her neck. I lead her to the SUV. She quickly jumped into the front seat—like she'd been jumping into that front seat her whole life. I went out back and told them I was taking her with me. Roberta shrugged. There were very few people actually living in the town, so no one was going to come looking for her. And as far as they were concerned, it was one less dog to feed or clean up after.

I wasn't sure if I would be back when I drove away that day, unsure of what awaited me in New Orleans. I had made few friends. The firemen were supportive and accommodating, but anyone associated with the shelter avoided me when they were there. The occasional visit by a local or friends of the staff eyed me suspiciously. Larry and I had continued to work together, but while I hustled in the humidity and heat, Larry followed me around like a lost puppy. It was as if he was training at a new job and wasn't quite sure what to do. The REMA folks and their generosity of spirit gave me hope. Without them, that first day would have been much, much harder. But as the miles fell behind me, I became more and more convinced that the Waveland Animal Shelter hadn't seen the last of me. Honey napped on the passenger seat, and my mind recalled the last few days—the people I had met and the animals I had tried to help. Dr. Broome and the vet students and Eric and Christy. Heather and the REMA folks with their colorful clothes and compassion, their eagerness to help the animals. The firefighters offered a stark contrast to the feelings I got when I was around the shelter staff. Tony, a guy I felt friendship with from the start, was a warm reminder of my time.

I saw the Aussie's scared little face and wondered what would become of her now. The kittens and the lack of care their litter box received, and who would clean their water bowls and give them fresh water? Who would care enough to bring the dogs outside for fresh air or keep them away while their kennels were cleaned? The Waveland Animal Shelter had been declared a condemned building, yet animals were still living in there. Nothing and no one should have been living or working in that shelter. The puppies were held and bathed, and when one of them pooped, I immediately cleaned it up. And every night before I crawled into the back of the SUV, I replaced all of the towels and blankets that were the only thing between them and the dirty, cold concrete.

Leaving Waveland, Mississippi, behind broke my heart.

I wound my way through the busted up neighborhoods and headed back to the main road headed west. I decided to avoid the interstate for a while and take the secondary roads. A highway sign indicated I was forty-nine miles from New Orleans, and I felt my heart leap in my chest. I was finally going to the city I had never visited, but loved.

As the miles fell away in my rearview mirror, tears welled in my eyes. I mistakenly believed I was driving away forever. That I had done all that I could. But the experience followed me. The images of the animals locked in cages. The stories of those that had drowned because they'd been left when the hurricane threatened. The puppies standing on barren concrete floors. The gutters filled with excrement and the smell—I'll never forget the smell. Mold, mildew, urine, and death all rolled up into one.

The sun was lowering in the western sky when I hit the I-10. As each mile brought me closer to New Orleans, I naïvely believed that the "real" Hurricane Katrina animal rescue experience awaited. New Orleans received the bulk of the hurricane media coverage, and it saw the most animal rescue and humanitarian efforts as well. Sadly, Mississippi was forgotten and largely ignored after the hurricane. And, try as I might, when I left Waveland I took it with me. Within my first few minutes since departure, I realized there was no turning my back on the place.

I had no idea what to expect when I arrived in New Orleans. I didn't even know where I was going. I kept hearing about Jane Garrison's group in the Garden District, and it seemed that of all the folks rescuing in New Orleans, they were the ones making the most impact and drawing the most attention. That's where I wanted to be. But I didn't know how to get to the Garden District, and even if I did, I had no idea how to find them once I was there. They had no address. In New Orleans, finding people was no longer a simple matter.

When I hit the outer limits of the city, I found myself trailing an eighteen-wheeler in the center lane. After a few miles, he pulled right to exit the highway, and I was directly behind a white cargo van with the words "Animal Rescue" painted on its back windows. What a welcome sight that beat-up van was! Figuring I had nothing to lose, I decided to follow it.

For six miles, I followed that white van. It pulled off at the St. Charles Avenue exit, and I followed. I kept on them as we weaved our way through a desolate but mostly intact section of the city. There was no electricity in New Orleans, and wooden sawhorses with stop signs marked significant intersections. Most of the buildings I passed were boarded up and vacant. There were very few cars on the streets and fewer pedestrians. Ignoring the "One Way" sign, the van turned left onto Felicity Street, and I did the same. A few blocks up, the van pulled over into a parking lot filled with SUVs, RVs, pickup trucks, and people. Honey and I pulled in behind them.

Two smiling women exited the van and approached me. One of the women wore an oversized T-shirt and jeans, and her hair was pulled back in a tight ponytail. Its end stuck out of a baseball cap. She introduced herself as "Wendy from Massachusetts," and I just about fell over. When the second woman joined us, a skeptical look on her face, Wendy introduced her as "Janice from Vermont." Overjoyed, I told them that I was "Chris from Massachusetts." Janice asked if I had been following them.

"Yes," I said. "I'm trying to find Jane's Garrison's group."

They both looked at each other and smiled. "This is it," they said.

Chapter Two

Beginnings

G rowing up, we always had cats. I can still remember the day I awoke to find our cat had given birth to kittens in the deep recesses of our front hallway closet, and I couldn't wait to climb in there to see them. In the darkness of that closet, the tiny little fur balls were nursing, and for weeks, my younger brothers, sister, and I respected their privacy, coming to name two of them "Pussghetti" and "Pussmato." Why those names I don't know, but I think it may have had something to do with my baby sister, Althea. When they were old enough to be away from their mom, they slept with me in my small twin-sized bed, made much smaller by their little round bodies nestled up close to my legs and curled into my back. I wouldn't move all night for fear they'd awaken and leave me. I remember the night I awoke to a warm feeling at the top of my head, cascading down to my ears. One of the kittens who had been sleeping on my pillow decided they didn't want to find the litter box. The next morning, we threw out the pillow and shortly after that started finding them new homes. It wasn't hard to do. Neighbors and friends of my mom and dad couldn't wait to get one of the little kittens.

One by one, I watched as they were carried away. I cried when it was time to say goodbye.

It wasn't until my early thirties that a dog came into my life and, try as I might to insist they were "too dependent" or "too needy," my then-partner Sally got her way, and a black cocker spaniel we named Whitney came home with us. Whitney was in a cage at the pet store in the local mall, a silky black cocker spaniel that the staff was eager to show us. I wanted nothing to do with that store or a dog, their sad little faces staring out of too-small cages, but a few minutes later Sally found me in the aisles and bounding with excitement insisted I go with her to see Whitney in the "get to know you room." When we walked into the room, Whitney was cowering in the corner staring at us with fearful eyes. The staff person told us a sad story about Whitney being returned. I immediately dropped to my knees and reached out to her shaking small body. The staff person knew good hearts when she saw them, and within minutes, we knew we couldn't leave the small, terrified little puppy behind. I'll never forget how Whitney shook when we carried her to the car, scared, vulnerable, reluctantly trusting, a little pink bow fastened to her head. A few weeks later, I cried when Sally clipped one of Whitney's nails too short, and her yelp and the subsequent bleeding brought out a homicidal maniac in me. I never let Sally touch Whitney's nails again.

Within a few months, a darling little sheltie we named Shelby followed. A purchase from that same mall pet store. Constant diarrhea and an overall sickly demeanor worried us, and frequent trips to the vet revealed a nasty bout with intestinal worms. On the way home from one of these visits, she defecated all over the back seat of my brand-new Honda Prelude. I remember pulling to the side of the road, feeling my rage escalate as I sought to find something, anything to clean the mess. Little Shelby sensed I was mad. She lay against the far door, her eyes sheepishly looking to mine. I knew so little then about the things in life that mattered. That puppies with severe diarrhea are really sick and car seats are not important. Fifteen months later, she was gone. The worms were eventually treatable, but fetal kidneys, due to irresponsible breeding from a "USDA-approved" breeding operation in Omaha, Nebraska—the beginning of my education about puppy mills—led to her untimely death. Sally and I did all we could, even teaching Shelby to use a litterbox given her constant need to urinate and inability to hold her urine for long due to her fetal-sized kidneys. We consulted specialists and homeopathic veterinarians, but nothing could be done. I remember taking her outside one night, holding her tight in my arms as I looked to the stars in the dark night sky, tears streaming down my face, praying that we would get a miracle and that Shelby would not leave me. Helplessly, naïvely hoping my love could save her.

Four months later, having ended my relationship with Sally, and suffering the loss of my dad and dearest Shelby, Sally and I decided that Whitney and our newest addition Shaney, another little sheltie, this time from a local breeder, would stay behind with her. Leaving the relationship was tough, but leaving the dogs was tougher. Five months after the breakup, and seeking to fill the holes left in my life, another little sheltie came into my life, my little Macy.

These were the days before I knew anything about kill shelters or pet overpopulation. I still believed, naïvely, as it was, that all cats were loved and had sweet little litters in hall closets, and the kittens were adopted to the neighbors. Macy came to me from a breeder in central Massachusetts, and I thought nothing of it when I was greeted at the door by five barking shelties, a few of them "breeding dogs." Macy was the smaller one in the back trying desperately to get my attention by jumping on the backs of the other more assertive dogs, and when I was finally able to sit down at the kitchen table, she jumped right into my lap—like she'd done it a hundred times before. I knew right then she was mine.

I grew up thirteen miles west of Boston in the old mill town of Waltham, Massachusetts. We were a sports-minded home where the TV was often tuned to the hometown teams. My mom, a waitress, worked nights, and my dad worked a variety of jobs until he landed a maintenance position at the new Marriott hotel in nearby Newton. My dad was the guy who could fix anything and make something out of nothing. At the Marriott, he was known by everyone for his charming gift of gab, and he quickly became the one who fixed the air conditioning, plowed the parking lot, and took care of the affluent elderly visitors who sometimes stayed for weeks or months on end. He was the unofficial expert on the company retirement plan, and everyone from the kitchen staff to the concierge consulted dad about everything Marriott.

My dad had a big heart and a liking for beer. My first sips came while running to the refrigerator to "get him another" while he sat in front of the TV every night. I liked beer, and it wasn't hard to notice that my extended family became much more fun during holiday visits after they had had a few drinks in them. And every single one of them did. In our family you drank.

By the age of eight, I was smoking cigarettes, and by twelve, I was drinking any form of alcohol I could get my hands on. Pot and drugs were soon to follow. They made me feel like someone I wanted to be. No longer the quiet, athletic tomboy with the too-short hair, I became the life of the party. My lack of self-confidence disappeared when I was drunk or stoned, and I no longer was the little girl, the neighborhood kids jokingly called "Piss" to rhyme with my shortened name, Chris. I loved making my friends laugh at the expense of myself. I craved the attention after twelve years of having little—the years of being trapped inside a voiceless kid shell. I drank and drugged with a vengeance, my first blackout coming through a bottle of gin that my cousin and I hijacked from my Yiayia's liquor cabinet. We took out two of her tall glasses and filled them with gin. Passing out, I awoke the next morning having no recollection of what happened after taking that first gulp. That blackout made me think I had done something "right."

In my neighborhood, I was the resident tomboy. A gifted athlete picked on by all, but one of the first chosen when we made baseball, hockey, or football teams of neighborhood kids. At the age of five, I found myself in the basement of our home in the hands of a sexual predator who liked them young. I had been playing with my dolls alone in the backyard, when a strange man approached. He pulled a handful of coins out of his pants pocket. I was mesmerized by the shiny quarters the most. He asked where I lived. He held my hand as I showed him.

I don't know how much time passed before mom called my dad and the police. My mom paced while we awaited their arrival. She seemed mad, and I thought I'd done something wrong. I remember the responding police officer with his hat in his hands and his dark uniform. It had shiny bright buttons. He sat in the corner chair of our living room and took notes in a small white lined notebook. Years later, having experienced an emotional breakdown at eight years sober and locked in a ward for survivors of sexual abuse, I relived the entire attack watching my tiny five-year-old girl in her favorite blue dress from the cellar ceiling of my childhood home.

The night of the flashback began like every other evening at the treatment center. We had dinner and our nightly meeting. By 8:00 p.m., our therapeutic day over, the twelve of us were sitting in the common area, a living room of sorts, and we were talking and laughing with one another. About an hour later, one of the nurses told us someone had been admitted. She had made a suicide attempt and was on the way from the hospital to our ward. It wasn't long after that I heard the large automated doors open, and two police officers escorted a stretcher down the long hallway in front of us. As soon as I saw their uniforms, I could feel myself growing uncontrollably angry. How dare they invade my safe place.

My rage came out of nowhere. I got up and went to my room. My roommate had gone to bed, and the lights were off. I got undressed in the dark. My hands were shaking. I laid down on the bed, and within seconds I felt my feet go numb. The numbness slowly crept up my legs and quickly found its way to my arms and hands. I didn't know what the hell was happening, but I was paralyzed. When it reached my throat and wound its way to my head, I suddenly saw myself fly through the air as my mom grabbed my hand. I had shown her my tiny fistful of shiny quarters. She asked where I got them, and I told her the man in the basement. When she grabbed my hand to take us down the dark stairs, I watched as my feet left the kitchen floor. She wasn't mad, my mom. She was scared. But I didn't know that when I was growing up all those years ago. I was certain what happened was my fault, and I blamed myself for the attack. I couldn't understand why I hadn't stopped him. And there I was in that treatment center, lying in my darkened room, on that locked ward, watching the whole attack unfold from the ceiling of the basement.

I was so little.

And he was so big.

It wasn't until I was thirty-three years old that I understood it wasn't my fault. When I was released from the treatment center, my dad and I talked about it for the first time. They never found the man. I didn't know any of that until we talked. It was the first time that day had ever been mentioned. My dad remembered everything. He told me the police left our home after the report was filed, and they rounded up a few child molesters known to them. They then brought them to my house. My parents would bring me to the front window to look out as they perp-walked my street. When that failed to elicit a response from me, they took my dad and me for a ride around my hometown, me in my dad's arms in the back seat of the cruiser. They were looking for "him." All I could see out the window was the blue sky above.

I remember that, late that night, I was shipped off to my grandparent's house. My papou, Peter, picked me up and we stopped at the Rexall drugstore on the way to my grandparents' home. I was, once again, in the back seat, although this time alone. I remember skootching myself up to peer out the window as he walked inside. I remember wondering if my parents had told him what had happened to me.

Soon after, my hair got cut short. A "pixie" cut it was called. Now I was not only good at sports, but I looked like a boy too. We played baseball out in front of our house, our street a dead end. In the winter, we carried our skates and ice hockey sticks down to the playground at the local elementary school. We even had a neighborhood street hockey league. I was the only girl. They put me in goal because it was the least glamorous position, but I was good at stopping the hard rubber puck, and one year I got the best player award. I loved cruising the streets of Waltham on my lime green Stingray bike with the banana seat and Mickey Mantle baseball cards pinned to my spokes with wooden clothespins. Anyone who knows anything about baseball cards or Mickey Mantle knows that years later, I could have sold those cards for thousands of dollars.

One day I was at the local kid pool. The kind that's no more than two feet deep with a water fountain in the middle. It was summer and sunny, and the water refreshingly cool, when my classmate Gil Manson picked up my cherished lime-green Stingray and threw it into a massive puddle of mud. And he laughed. And all the kids laughed. I gathered up my towel, pleading with my seven-year-old eyes not to cry. I walked my mud-soaked bike all the way home and told my mom. She wanted to know where the MANSON family lived. We got in the car and drove down the hill to the pool. Gil lived right across the street. My mom was short on nurture but long on protection. She was pissed. No one was going to mess with her kid. I sat in the car while she knocked on the front door. I hid in the front seat. As much as I liked mom sticking up for me, I feared it would only make matters worse. Gil's sister Joanne answered the door. She was one of the bigger kids in the neighborhood, and she had been scaring me for years with her sarcasm, large frame, and strutting stride. I saw her look to the car, her curly brown hair a menacing sight. I remember she smirked.

In junior high, I started to smoke pot and drink alcohol on the way to school every day. I skipped classes and raided the medicine cabinets at my friends' houses when they threw parties.

It didn't matter what the bottle read, if they were pretty and plentiful, I took them. At fourteen, I swallowed a handful of my mom's Percocet. I slept for twenty hours. It was a half-hearted attempt to sleep forever.

I lived for summer, where I excelled in the softball field, and at thirteen, a girl's ice hockey team formed in my town. I showed up to the first practice with my street hockey mask and my white figure skates. It was all I had. Coach threw his son's old and worn-out goalie equipment on me, and for the next five years, I played ice hockey on one of the first girl's ice hockey teams in the United States. Ice hockey quite possibly saved my life by giving me the first thing I was really good at. And while the drugs and alcohol were my daily MO, I somehow managed borderline grades and graduated to high school.

High school was, well . . . high. The curriculum got harder, and so did the drugs. I was an equal opportunity garbage head. Pot, booze, and my mom's Percocet's no longer did the trick. Enter my first acid trip—a hit of windowpane sophomore year. I watched the numbers jump off the classroom clock in third period English and become a numbered marching band around the room. Aghast, I looked away. I looked at my English teacher and watched as her face melted—all over her shirt falling in gooey drops of face on the floor at her feet, where it pooled and looked up at me. That freaked me out too, so I put my head down on the desk where the single sheet of paper became cluttered with bright red puckered lips that stuck their tongues out at me. Rows of tongues mocking me.

It was a nightmare. And while the trip that day did not get any better, I'll never understand how someone didn't notice when I walked the halls between classes like I was walking in quicksand. Which, unbeknownst to me at the time, I was. My friend Deb Jones was at my side, asking me, "What the hell was

I doing?" All the strange faces were watching and laughing. And watching. And laughing. Deb's 100 percent lucid brain took over, and she brought me to the cafeteria. Where a few hundred creatures of various heights and sizes seemed to watch every step I took.

Food. I needed food. I thought it would help me to come down. So I asked Deb to get me one of those packaged ice cream cones with the flat crunchy chocolate with peanuts on top. I started to open it and watched it crumble in my hands. I yelled at her. "Why the hell did you get me a broken one?!" at the top of my lungs. Heads turned. It felt like the entire cafeteria was looking at me. Like time had stopped. I was losing my mind and bolted to the girl's room. I slammed myself in a stall. Deb followed. She asked me to open the door, but when I stood to touch the door, both arms were swallowed whole by it. And, as I stood there with my arms seemingly stuck in the door, I screamed.

The rest of that awful day is lost to me. I know I spent most of it in that girl's room, but I have no memory of the bus ride home. What I do remember is hanging out at the ice rink that night. I was still so high from the acid, but the hallucinations had stopped. I remember feeling elated and light, higher than I had ever felt, but in a wondrous and delightful way.

A week later, I did it again.

The summer after high school graduation, I drove an ice cream truck. And while I saw the immediate benefit of having several cubic square feet of a motorized cooler, my parents held little appreciation for my entrepreneurial spirit. I think they wanted more of an effort on my part to secure adequate employment. And the truck required plugging in at night. The electric bill was a concern.

I had been accepted for fall admission to the local community college, which was nothing to really brag about. They took everyone within a 100-mile radius. Woefully unprepared for adulthood and lacking any viable employment skills, I kept the truck.

On weekends my friends and I would load up the coolers with beer and find a nice spot to park and drink. Usually, we'd hang out at the local softball field where we played our games. An ice cream truck parked at the field, even without a game that night, seemed to draw little attention.

Alcohol and drugs offered temporary relief from the sadness of my life, but they destroyed any hope I had at forming meaningful relationships. I picked people who hurt me. My version of "bad boy" syndrome had a twist. At fifteen, I kissed a girl. Let's call her Ellen. We fell in serious love and hid from the world. It was 1974, and we thought we were "faggots." It was the only language we had. Ellen and I lived thirteen miles away, so weekend sleepovers were the only time we saw each other. During the week, we'd write long love letters to one another, and on the weekend, we'd share our words of adoring love. When she ran away from home, I burned them all. Her parents had found out about us and grounded her. They forbade her ever to see me again. Years later, I would think of those letters of first love and regret that they were gone.

When her parents found out about our illicit relationship, Ellen was so despondent she ran away from home, first faking her drowning in the reservoir down the street from her house. She didn't want anyone looking for her. That night she showed up at my softball game and called my name while hiding in the woods in center field. Her parents were at the game because they had come looking for me. They hated me. My teammates and I hid her that night at a friend's house, but two days later, during a softball tournament in a nearby town, her parents unexpectedly showed up. Ellen was sitting in the stands, and when her dad exited their car, he came right towards me. Her dad was a large man, but when he tried to get close to me, my teammates stood in his way. He went to the stands and grabbed her by the arm. She was screaming and resisting when he picked her up and threw her over his shoulders. He carried her like that all the way to their car, her fists pummeling his back. I didn't see her again for weeks.

Ellen was a nice girl. Barring the night she stole money out of the cash box at a local restaurant where a bunch of us had just had dinner. We ran screaming from the restaurant when she reached into the cash drawer. Or when she robbed a gas station somewhere between Florida and Massachusetts while transporting kilos of cocaine that had arrived in stuffed animals from Columbia. In our early twenties, she had enough blow to cover New England in a few inches of near 100 percent pure Columbian-pink.

I was attracted to people who tended to disappoint. The unavailable. The ones who already *had* a girlfriend. Or an edge. They drank and took drugs like I did. We went out dancing and got blotto'ed and woke the next day in our night-before clothes, not knowing where the car was. Or who had driven home. I dropped out of community college after a month when it became apparent the only curriculum I was excelling at was playing kitty whist in the cafeteria. The ice cream truck long gone I had to find full-time work. The local state hospital needed workers. Positions were plentiful, and when offered to decide between the higher functioning residents or the severely disabled and bedridden, I chose the latter. The most vulnerable pulled at me.

I was twenty-four when I found myself in an AA meeting, surrounded by 100 or so sober women, all of them looking like damn movie stars, and me hiding out in the back row, two seats down from a nurse I worked with at that state hospital. She had been a steady supply of drugs from day one, and there we were sitting feet apart in the same damn row of an AA meeting. That was inconvenient. I went to AA to stop using coke. The control I thought I had over alcohol and drugs was smashed when I stuck my nose in white power. That shit had to go. But I had no intention *whatsoever* of stopping drinking or taking drugs. It was coke. Coke was the problem.

But that night I caught something. Hope. And with a pocketful of phone numbers, all I wanted was more. Leaning against a bannister while everyone filed out I did the next illogical thing and invited everyone back to my small apartment in Somerville. I didn't know what those women had, but I wanted it too. So, when they laughed and invited me out to the S&S Restaurant in Cambridge for "fellowship and tea" . . . Wait—what? Well, I went. And I just kept going.

Sobriety scooped me up and carried me. Raw, hopeless at times, I didn't do coke. Or drugs or alcohol. My parents had long since divorced, and a seven-month Computer Hardware course had given me a foundation in the lucrative high-tech field. I surrounded myself with sober people and got a good therapist. At five years of sobriety, I began rebuilding a relationship with my dad. For years every night when I came home, he'd be drinking on the back porch. And when sleeping on the living room couch had become an embarrassment to us all he made that porch his bedroom and TV and drinking room. He'd often be so drunk he didn't see that I was too. He'd talk and talk, and I'd sit just sit there. Sometimes, my eyes heavy, I'd be calling on every ounce of patience to sit and listen because I knew he had no one else to talk to but me.

My dad loved to talk. At ten years sober, he was diagnosed with lung cancer, which quickly spread to his bones. The day before he died, I visited him at his house in Newton. I knew it was the end. His living room looked like a hospital room. The room where I had spent many a joyous Christmas was now a room of death and dying. The Christmas tree had been taken down a few months prior. The lights packed away for another year. Where the tree once stood, there was a hospital bed. A stainless steel tray held cotton balls that my stepmother used to lovingly wet my father's parched lips. I was moved to tears when she told me that.

As I sat next to his bed and waited for him to open his eyes, I realized I had no idea what to expect if he did. He looked much different than just a few weeks prior when he was lying in a sunlit hospital room with my brother Bill by his side. Together they were watching a Red Sox game on TV. My big, strong brother looked so small and helpless to me that day, sitting next to my father. He was leaning forward, straining to hear every word my dad spoke, his hands clasped together in a giant fist. I knew that feeling too. The feeling of not wanting to miss something. Of holding on tight to each word that passed between my father and me. As if hunting and gathering, my father's words would somehow keep him alive just a little bit longer. It was a preseason game. Spring training: the season of new beginnings. The trees were beginning to blossom, the crocuses peeking their tiny, little heads from beneath their winter berth. My dad seemed in such good spirits that day. The pain, which had racked his body for weeks, had granted him a reprieve. I recall talking to a nurse on the floor about how happy he seemed. And I remember her reply: "He looks awful to me. I think the cancer has gone to his brain. It's spreading." I was devastated as I walked away. Pissed, she tainted the illusion.

There was no sunlight in dad's living room the last time I saw him alive. The shades are drawn, the TV off. It was just my father and me. I saw a bleached white, starving leg peeking out from under the starched white sheet, and I was embarrassed and saddened. My father, so tall, so strong, had been reduced to a skeleton of a human being. When his eyes opened, I jumped from the couch next to his bed. I wanted him to know he wasn't alone. I wanted him to know that I was there. I reached over the bed rail to touch his hand. It lay limp in mine, weightless, and his eyes glazed, staring straight ahead, as if he were watching a distant movie just over my shoulder for an audience of one. "I love you, Dad. It's OK. I know you have to go. You've been the best father, and I'm going to miss you so much, but I'll be OK." I don't know if he heard me. All I know is a small sound escaped from his throat, and I felt the slightest little movement of his hand in mine. It would be the last time I saw my father alive.

I met some bad girls in AA too, but at eight years sober, I broke the streak, and I met Sally. We both shared a love of books, jogging, and working out at the gym, and within a year, we moved in together. She was the most beautiful skier I had ever seen take to the slopes, and during the winters, we traveled to Vermont and Maine to ski the east. And were it not for her I would have never met the loves of my life.

It was 1995 when I found my little Macy. I don't know the exact moment she cracked open my heart, but it was most likely on the ride home that very first day. I got behind the wheel, and once again, she jumped into my lap and stayed there the entire way. Macy made it known from the start that I was hers, and that was that.

For the next year and a half, it was just the two of us sharing my two-bedroom loft in the Central Square neighborhood of Cambridge. My twelve-year stint of severe drinking and cocaine addiction, which led to two serious suicide attempts, were behind me now, and at twelve years sober I had picked up the pieces of my fractured life and built a successful information technology consulting business. Every failed relationship made me realize I was better off alone, and when I got lonely, it was Macy, riding shotgun in the car, that I talked to. Daily walks exploring the neighborhoods of Cambridge and leisurely visits to the bookstores of Harvard Square were our routine, and on long walks when I sensed her little legs growing tired, I would pick her up and carry her home. In her company, I experienced peace and perfect love.

A year and a half later, I heard of another sheltie at Macy's breeder who had "failed" at being a show dog and needed a home. And on a cold and snowy November night, Macy and I went and picked up Demi. When I got her home, the two of them ran in the freshly falling snow, in the tiny postage-stamp-sized backyard of my loft in Cambridge, and I knew then my decision to get us another dog had been a good one. For the next twelve years, Macy and Demi were my "Team Sheltie."

It might have been the honesty and vulnerability I saw in their eyes. It could have been the way they jumped into the car without thinking twice—just knowing wherever I was taking them was going to be a safe and good place. Maybe it was the way they would get so excited at the thought of dinnertime, the knowledge I acquired, gradually, that they depended on me, on *me*. That every day was filled with love, comfort, and food. That every time I walked in the door; it was as if they hadn't seen me in years.

They made me human. It wasn't my parents, or schooling, my career, or a church. No spirituality or therapy or even AA meetings were responsible for my development into a good person—a kind person, forgiving, and humble. It was my Team Sheltie that taught me all of that. They were my first pack, and we spent our days understanding each other in the silences between us. Knowing the unspoken language of perfect love. That even when I tripped on being human and got mad at them for silly things like barking too much or eating the money I left out for the housecleaner, that even then all was forgiven, all was OK, I was human, so what.

When Macy's health began to fail, my heart shuttered in my chest. Like swallowing the pit of a peach, I carried a lump in my throat that I knew would suffocate me when she died. As I watched her steps slow and her eyes begin to fade, I dared to believe again that maybe my love could save her.

The day the end came, I asked my vet to please come to the house. It was an early evening in late March, and the darkness and cold were still holding on in Boston. My little Macy lay on the king-sized bed with me by her side. Her breathing labored, I touched her soft fur, looked into her dimming eyes, and spoke the last words I would ever say to her, assuring her she could go, that I'd be OK—not for a moment believing I would. As I watched her take her last breath, a sound escaped from my chest and echoed through the room. I wrapped Macy in a blanket and carried her to the car, holding her close to my chest, my eyes a waterfall of grief. For weeks, I couldn't breathe. I cried so hard, sometimes falling to the floor in a small mountain of despair.

Three months later, my Demi left me as well. And I knew it was because I was not the only one of us who loved Macy.

Chapter Three

NOLA

New Orleans. Two months post-Katrina. I had made it. I couldn't believe my luck to find myself with Jane Garrison's group. Animal Rescue New Orleans (ARNO), informally known as "Jane Garrison's group," was operating out of an abandoned dry cleaner/nail salon, which trisected Felicity, Magazine, and Richard streets in the Lower Garden District. The building was mostly intact, but the roof had suffered severe wind damage. When it rained, a daily occurrence for New Orleans in late summer, it leaked. Badly.

By October, emergency generators provided most of the electricity in New Orleans. Our operations lacked such luxuries, so flashlights and headlamps supplied the only available light. An overgrown and vacant lot next door was dotted with tents and the parking lot around the building was filled with SUVs, cargo vans, pickup trucks, and for a few lucky folks, large RVs. Our sole source of water was an outside spigot from the building across the street, but for the sturdy souls who traveled to New Orleans to help the animals, this place became home.

Folks had come from all over the western hemisphere: vet techs from Mexico and veterinarians from Maine, animal control officers from Washington State, and search and rescue teams from Colorado. Cadi Schiffer, a short-in-stature, cat-loving brunette from Vancouver, was coordinating the feeding and watering stations distributed throughout Orleans Parish, and Holly Quaglia from Virginia was one of two site coordinators. We were men and women, young and older, and on any given day, our numbers fluctuated, depending on who had arrived and who had returned home. There was one thing we all had in common: we wanted to do something to help the animals of New Orleans.

The isolation I felt during my time in Waveland quickly disappeared. In New Orleans, I was surrounded by others trying to figure out the whole mess. Honey Bear was an instant hit. By now, our relationship so casual people wondered if I'd brought her with me from home. Everyone wanted to hear about the Mississippi Gulf Coast and were aghast when I told them about Waveland's conditions. Surrounded by allies and like-minded people, I jumped in with both feet and got to work. First, I had to meet the coordinators. Was Jane there? Janis and Wendy began introducing me to people, and I learned that two folks—Rob from Louisiana and Holly from Virginia—were the unofficial coordinators. Waveland's animals couldn't be forgotten, and I'd need more help and resources to save them. Having a satellite-connected laptop increased my popularity considerably and gave me instant credibility. There were little to no internet connections before my arrival, and Rob and Holly needed my help too.

There were a lot of people on Magazine that first day. Everyone had a purpose and seemed to know exactly what to do. Vehicles continually filed in and out, and folks unloaded large bags of pet food or setup crates. Some tightened or strung sheets through trees that were used to create shade to protect the animals from the relentless sun. Others were busy filling out paperwork. There were stacks upon stacks of donated warm vitamin water, all the same—bright red, Power-C, dragon fruit. It was the only thing we had to drink.

My first priority was to get some of the Waveland animals "pulled." "Pulled" is a term used in animal rescue that means to get an animal out of a potentially life-threatening situation. I'd started to learn the lingo. I was mostly concerned for Petey because I had been told the Waveland Animal Shelter did not adopt pit bulls. That he was still alive was nothing short of a miracle, and it felt urgent I get him out first. And while I was concerned about all the animals in Waveland, Petey and the terrified Aussie Shepard became my priorities. If I could only pull a few at a time, they would go first.

On my first day, I familiarized myself with my surroundings and built a relationship with Holly and Rob. That first night in New Orleans, when the humidity had dropped slightly and the evening sky turned a pastel shade of purplish-blue, I was lying in the back of the Sequoia with Honey Bear by my side when my cell phone rang. It was Peg Milner from Washington State, a onetime resident of Waveland. She had left Waveland six years prior to escape an ex-husband who had threatened to kill her. She was friends with Connie and offered to help in any way she could. We talked for well over an hour. Peg was intimately familiar with the Waveland shelter. For decades concerned citizens hoped for a shelter where their communities' animals were safe. But the Waveland Animal Shelter was a house of horrors, and it had no support from town officials. The apathy the animal rescue community had witnessed firsthand was systemic—it had nothing to do with the storm. After shutting down my phone for the night, I cracked the windows and hugged Honey to my side. It was the first decent sleep I'd had since arriving on the Gulf Coast.

Morning broke, and I rolled out of the Sequoia and gently nudged Honey Bear outside. After a short walk, we got back to the parking lot and watched the others come in from the tents and climb down out of the RVs. Each day began with a 7:00 a.m. meeting. We would circle around the large map of New Orleans that was covered in little yellow Post-it notes. Each yellow square had two names, identifying the team responsible for that area. Holly stood on a chair and addressed the crowd. There were food and watering stations that had to be checked, and new neighborhoods searched. Trapping teams were formed, and some volunteered to stay behind to check in the animals brought in all day long. The veterinarians formed their own group and would work inside the building where the rooms had crates and bedding for the wounded or sick. Everyone was there to work.

Once assigned a teammate and a feeding station, I walked Honey Bear around the corner to an open vet clinic. They were going to keep her for the day so she could be checked out and vaccinated. I asked them to please give her whatever she needed.

I spent that first day in Mid-City restocking the feeding stations with a guy from the Pacific Northwest. We had a paper map of the city, and the back of the SUV was filled with bags of pet food and gallon bottles of water we filled from the spigot next door. We wouldn't return until we'd run out of supplies, and if anyone of us spotted loose animals, we had a number to call to give the location and description of the stray animal. Jane Garrison kept a list of those sightings, so when the sky grew dark, the trappers could go out and look for them. The animals were typically more active at night as they felt safer under the cover of darkness.

Magazine Street is usually a bustling stretch of restaurants, storefronts, galleries, and coffee shops, but in late October 2005, New Orleans was a forsaken and desolate city. A few businesses had reopened and provided us a gas station, Mexican burrito joint, True Value Hardware, and, fortunately, one of New Orleans's best coffee shops, Rue de la Course. It was enough to keep our weary band of warriors fed and caffeinated, and it sure beat the lone Sonic in Waveland. My first full day's excitement was extinguished as soon as I started driving through the neighborhoods east and north of the Garden District.

Whole sections of the city were gone.

It was destroyed. The only vehicles on the street were the military, utilities, the police, or us. Very few residents had come back. For miles in every direction, whole blocks of homes and businesses lay in ruins. Heaping piles of debris lined the roads. Refrigerators stood sentry in front of almost every house; some with their doors flung open, their colorful magnets still attached to their outsides. Many had been spray-painted with nasty messages for FEMA or the US government while others had been decorated and draped in Mardi Gras beads. Their most compelling feature was their smell. It was the worst stench I'd ever been exposed to.

We drove down one-way streets with no working traffic signals and wind-tossed street signs littering median strips. We pulled U-turns, tires screeching if we spotted a dog or cat. It felt like the set of a dystopian movie, where only a few living beings had survived. It was a sharp contrast to what I had imagined it would be. The colors, sights, and sounds evoked in James Lee Burke's prose had created a sultry city of life, color, music, and lush vegetation. There was nothing that could have prepared me for the things I saw.

That first day we drove the streets refilling water bowls and large disposable lasagna pans with dog and cat food. When we ran out of the pans, we'd slice open an entire bag of food and leave it on the ground. The animals left signs of their presence: empty food and water containers, or small paw prints in the mud or dust. Most houses were spray-painted with the universal search and rescue X's that revealed the date they were searched. A few homes had longer messages indicating cats or dogs were living somewhere nearby or had been taken from the house—or found dead inside.

We covered every street of greater New Orleans, Metairie, and Kenner. We traveled north to the lake and east to the Ninth Ward. We went as far as we could go before we hit the road-blocks of military vehicles. Every neighborhood had abandoned animals. We hoped they were still alive. By this time, most of the animals were now terrified of humans, the comfort and safety they once knew, gone. In some yards, there were dogs left alone in the back, chain-link fences keeping them in. But none were able to keep us out.

Sometimes the dogs would bark a warning for us to keep away, but mostly they just wandered up to the fence with a meek look of confusion on their faces. Those were some of the hardest to see because we couldn't take them with us. The best we could do was throw them some food and make sure they had fresh, clean water.

The coordinators at Magazine continued to update the feeding station locations. Many rescuers asked for the same neighborhoods to check on animals they had seen in yards or hiding under homes. It was increasingly difficult to not become attached. The trapping teams had their hands full, and it took a lot of time trying to lure the animals out from their hiding places. We didn't just feed and run. We searched and crawled and spoke in loving voices. Seeing them scared and hungry was too much for some. Holding each other up became part of the job. Seeing a previously rock-hard rescuer breakdown into tears chipped away at us all.

For this reason, no one went out on their own. The city was still a dangerous place. Curfews remained, and whole neighborhoods were off-limits to anyone except the police or animal control officers. Those neighborhoods worried us the most because stories quickly spread that the animals found by local law enforcement didn't make it out alive.

For most, the work was personal. Watching the helpless suffer was an injury many had experienced in their own lives. Everyone who went to New Orleans carried their own internal storms. Our shared histories compelled us to act and to protect and comfort the abandoned, opening our own wounds in the process. *We had to save the animals.*

After my partner and I checked the feeding stations in our section, we decided to drive downtown. I drove out to the I-10, the overhead highway that passed through much of downtown New Orleans. It was a graveyard of abandoned vehicles. Hundreds of deserted cars and trucks were gathered at the on-ramps and stuffed under overpasses. Many were simply left in the road. All were the color of Katrina gray. It was out by the I-10 that I first saw dead dogs. Some were on the road, but most were lying in the median strips—the hidden places in neighborhoods no longer hiding their death. They were in varying stages of decomposition. I quickly turned my head away. There was nothing we could do for them now.

Police or one of the few folks still living in the city would occasionally flag us down. Our non-Katrina gray SUVs, with the shoe-polish printed words "Animal Rescue" written on the back window, became welcome sights in dark and dreary neighborhoods. Many folks were desperate to locate their pets, having returned to the city in the hope of finding their beloved animal. Others just wanted someone to talk to, someone who would understand their grief because their animal had died. Many of them were racked with guilt that they didn't do more or take their animals with them. A few told us how they were forced, some at gunpoint, to leave their pets behind.

It was on one such stop that I met Manuel Williams. Driving through Central City one day with another volunteer named Xavier, we happened upon a man ripping the siding from a small shotgun house. He saw our vehicle and waved us down. I pulled over and rolled down my window. Manuel leaned in and started to talk.

When Katrina hit, he evacuated to the Superdome with his wife, child, and dog, a little chow named Missy. After a few days stranded at the dome, buses came to begin evacuating people. Manuel was told animals were not allowed on the buses; they would have to leave Missy behind. People had been put in impossible situations and given no options but the inconceivable. Manuel loved his dog and pleaded to be able to bring her on board. His pleas fell on deaf ears. He decided to put her in the cab of his pickup. He rolled down the windows and filled a large container with water, an opened bag of dog food laid out on the back seat. The military and law enforcement didn't tell folks where they were going, but he believed he'd be back in a few days. He boarded the bus and prayed she'd be OK. The bus didn't stop until Houston.

It would be the last time he would see Missy.

Now, two months later, he was still searching for her. He asked me if there was anything we could do. He told me he and his family hadn't been the same since they boarded that bus to a destination unknown. His wife and daughter were still in

Houston, and he had just returned to New Orleans that week. He came back for a job rebuilding a friend's home, and all he wanted was to find his dog. As he told me his story, he got choked up and couldn't talk anymore.

He paused and asked me to hold on.

I watched him walk over to a dust-covered, beat-up old pickup and reach inside through the driver's window. He came back and held out a photo. It was a small, creased picture of a little black dog. It was a picture of Missy. I looked at Manuel. He looked away. I saw him reach up with his right hand to pinch his eyes. Manuel was too proud to let me see him cry. I told him I would see what I could do, and I would meet him back there the next day. Xavier and I drove away. We were both crying for Manuel and for Missy. When I looked in my tear-filled rearview mirror, Manuel was standing in the middle of the street watching us drive away, a small photo in his hand.

That night the Best Friends panel truck showed up at Magazine like it did every night. No matter what we were doing at the time, we dropped everything so we could load up the animals. Every single one had medical or informational paper-work created for them, and a blanket put in their cage. Some had small plastic baggies filled with medication for the various injuries, infections, and skin conditions many had. Some of the volunteers were tasked with making sure every animal had information regarding where they had been found. Reuniting animals with their families was a priority even though getting them out of the city quickly was a necessity.

The truck pulled in, and we created a human chain. Every one of us would grab a side of a crate. We'd laugh and sing and talk to the animals as we loaded them onto the truck. Some of us cried as we said our goodbyes. Holly would jump in and ensure every crate and kennel was secured to the interior walls of the truck.

Large crates with the large dogs on the bottom and the smaller dogs in smaller crates on top. Some folks knelt in front of the crates reassuring the animals inside that they would be leaving now. Leaving the city that they had survived for months. No more foraging for food or fighting for survival. No more dodging deputies' bullets or showing face only at night. They were safe now. A check and recheck of the animals, and they were on their way to Tylertown, Mississippi, where Best Friends was running a shelter on land donated by the St. Francis Animal Sanctuary.

A professional couple displaced by the flood had rented an apartment across the street from us on Felicity. At night they'd watch us from their balcony. One night they decided to visit. They mentioned they had been watching us every night and calling us "Hound Zero." The name took.

That night, when everyone had cleaned and closed up Hound Zero, I pulled my SUV behind the dry cleaners' gates. A few dogs were sleeping comfortably in kennels outside under the tarps, and inside were several kittens too young or sick to send to Tylertown. I climbed into the back of the SUV with Honey. It was too hot to use my sleeping bag. Honey snuggled up next to me, and I pulled out my laptop and started my search for Missy.

My internet connection made me very popular on Magazine. It worked anywhere, thanks to the satellite card. An internet search for Missy turned up a picture of her tethered to a handrail outside of the Superdome. The photo had a tracking number associated with a database that a group of women called the "Stealth Volunteers" had been populating since the storm's earliest days. The Stealth Volunteers were a geographically dispersed group, primarily located in the United States and Canada. They were the ones who coordinated all of the calls from the multiple rescue groups working throughout the city and updated a database used to hopefully reunite animals with their people. I searched on Missy's name and her tracking number. Because of the picture, I knew someone had saved her. But every search came up empty. It was like Missy had been rescued and then disappeared. Rose, a woman from California, helped me research Missy's case. We spoke multiple times each day, but the news was always the same. Every lead on Missy's whereabouts turned up a dead end.

The Stealth Volunteers were the first to tell me about Ted and Judy Goncalves. Lifelong residents of New Orleans, they lived in a modest two-story home in the Lakeview section of New Orleans located just south of Lake Pontchartrain. They had two children and two dogs, Lucky and Nemo. Storm evacuations were not unique for the below-sea-level city residents, and they took in stride the warnings about Katrina. Judy took the kids and evacuated. Ted stayed in New Orleans with the dogs and reported to duty at the Superdome. He left them enough food and water for a few days and reported to duty. The family had mistakenly believed they'd be home in a day or two. Tops.

After working at the Superdome around the clock for two weeks and unable to get to his home in Lakeview, Ted returned on September 19. The flood had gutted his home. His animals were gone. The large spray-painted symbol on the front of the house indicated two animals had been found inside. There was no mention of who found them. There was no date either.

On a blistering hot November morning, I drove to Lakeview to meet them. Located north of downtown, it was a complicated maze to make my way to Lakeview. Most of the roads were impassable or downright dangerous to attempt. Many were permanently closed. Wooden sawhorses, jersey barriers, and dodging deep craters made the trip much longer than normal. I had their address and met them on Twenty-second Street. I arrived first. I parked in front of the jersey barrier that prevented me from driving to the end of their road. I'd have to walk to their home.

I walked a few blocks down the road, looking for something that might identify their house. I came upon a pile of moldy, mildewed possessions in front of a house with the giant "X" spray-painted on the mold-covered exterior. The home's numbers were still attached next to the opening for the door. The large pile out front consisted of family pictures in splintered frames and heaps of sunburnt clothes. Waterlogged and heat-soaked furniture, battered and broken, were tossed about, and there was a lot of broken glass. I heard a car, and it pulled up next to mine. A man exited the driver's side and started to walk my way. I smiled. He didn't. He looked tired and worn. I threw out my hand and introduced myself. When I looked back at their car, I saw a woman sitting in the passenger seat. She leaned a bit forward like she hadn't the strength to hold herself up. When she caught me looking, she quickly turned away.

"It's too hard for my wife," Ted said. "She's going to stay in the car."

I told him how sorry I was for the tragedy that had struck their family. Ted told me his story. He came back to his home at some point on September 19. He believed his dogs had been taken alive from the residence sometime the week prior. If they hadn't survived the flooding, their bodies would have been inside, and the symbol out front would have indicated 2 DOA. It appeared that Lucky and Nemo had survived the flood.

Ted held out a few pictures. "These were all I could find in what's left," he told me. I took them from his hands. The water damage made it hard to see them clearly. In one of the pictures,

Lucky was kissing Ted's daughter. The note on the bottom of the photograph said it had been taken on her fifteenth birthday. I told Ted I'd do everything I could to find his dogs. We agreed to meet back at the house in a few days.

That night I worked with a Stealth Volunteer to try to find Lucky and Nemo. I gave her as much information as I had for the Goncalves's family dogs. For the next few days, the volunteers exhausted every outlet available to them. Their search came up empty. No one would ever know what had become of the two dogs taken from Twenty-second Street in New Orleans. Once I knew there was nothing more we could do, I took the dreaded ride back to Twenty-second Street in Lakeview. I'd be the one to tell Ted and Judy that we didn't know what had become of their dogs. Well, I told Ned.

Judy never left the car.

Later that same day, I met Manuel at his friend's house. I wasn't sure how I would tell him I could not find his beloved Missy. I pulled up the picture I had found of Missy, and his face lit up, and he exclaimed in a perfect New Orleans dialect, "Dat's my dawg!" Missy had become a symbol for the many designated as "left behind," her picture on news websites. I searched for the words to tell him she hadn't been found, but that I had people looking for her. "But dat's a good sign, right, Miss Chris?" he asked. With some hesitation, I replied, "It is, Manuel—it's a good sign." As I drove away that day, I knew I had only been able to give Manuel a false sense of hope. The chances we would ever find Missy were not good.

My second full day in New Orleans began with a trip to Waveland. That morning, Rob and Holly had agreed to take in as many Mississippi dogs as I could bring back to Hound Zero. A few folks were lingering around, getting ready for the day, and I asked if anyone wanted to take a trip to Mississippi. A woman who introduced herself as "Barb" jumped at the offer. Barb was from San Diego, California, and had been in New Orleans for a few weeks. I told her why the trip was necessary and what we would be doing, and she asked if we'd need any supplies. We needed a larger vehicle than the Sequoia, so I asked Rob for suggestions. He offered his pickup truck that was outfitted with a cab and crates in the back.

On the road to Waveland, I tried to prepare Barb for what awaited us. The situation was dire in New Orleans, but our makeshift rescue center was a bubble of sorts that comforted and supported us. Our animals were well cared for and loved. More people arrived every day, and donations of pet food, medical supplies, and crates came in from all over the country. And we had significant support from Best Friends. Barb assured me she'd be OK, but she had tears in her eyes within minutes of arriving. She was shocked that the building we pulled up to had anything living in it at all. I asked her if we could take some time to walk the older dogs first because it was safe to assume they hadn't been since I'd left. She was happy to do it. We walked inside to the back where the office was located. The door between the kennel area and that room was closed tight. The dogs started barking immediately. We found the staff sitting around a small card table eating their takeout food from Sonic.

I told Roberta, Chase, Tori, and Larry that we were there to take some of the animals, and Roberta acknowledged my statement with barely a shrug. It was pretty clear they couldn't care less about what I did with the animals. Barb and I walked into the kennel area. The cages were disgusting. Feces and urine were smeared from the pads of little paws in every kennel, and there were no blankets, towels, or bedding. The water bowls were empty, and there were no food bowls in any of the cages. I looked into Petey's cage; his sad eyes barely acknowledged me. I told Barb he was the first we'd be loading up. His neck looked only marginally better than it had when I left. The Aussie was coming too. The progress we had made when Heather ran with her through the parking lot could not be for naught. Barb and I painstakingly chose dogs to pull that day. It was brutal deciding who would be lucky enough to come with us, and the faces of those we couldn't take haunted me. Roberta eventually came out back and showed us a litter of fifteen puppies brought in, and she told us she wanted them "gone." I could do that. I could make them gone. I promised Roberta that someone would be back the next day to get them.

We pulled seven dogs that trip: Petey, the Aussie, and five others. After walking all of them, we loaded up Rob's truck. Holly had told me before we left for Waveland that a few could go that night on the Best Friends transport. We focused on young adults and made our decisions quickly. Barb took a particular interest in an adorable little border collie, but we had run out of space. I promised her I'd get him out of there when I passed through on my way home.

With the animals safely loaded and an adorable yellow Lab in the cab with us, we headed back to New Orleans. A few miles into the trip, Barb let out a laugh and reached back between our seats. The Lab had poked up his head and smiled as the miles between him and Waveland grew further away. He stayed that way the entire ride to Magazine Street. Every few miles, I caught that smile in my rearview. Damn, that made me feel good.

When we hit Hound Zero, folks couldn't wait to help us unload the Waveland dogs. They ooh'ed and ahh'ed as they were taken off Rob's truck. A young couple from New York took an immediate liking to the smiling yellow lab, and they placed a lead around his neck and walked him into the staging area. Within the hour, they asked me if they could adopt him. They said they had been hoping for a dog just like him, and they had already given him a name. They named him Waverly because, mistaking Waveland for Waverly, they thought he was from Waverly, Mississippi. It was a fine name! Barb and I were so happy our smiling co-pilot had found a new home.

Once everyone had been unloaded, I was approached by one of the volunteers. From Washington State, Judy operated a small rescue, and she thought the Aussie and Petey would be great candidates to leave with her the next day. She told us they would easily find homes. At that moment, I was elated. I felt like I had unwittingly fallen into something. If I could just get the animals out of Waveland, they'd be OK. I wasn't sure how I'd do it, but I would. I'd pull as many as I could for as long as possible, and I wouldn't give the staff the chance to kill them. It was on that day that my life changed forever.

The next morning, once again I rolled off of my sleeping bag, grabbed a warm Power-C bottled water, and stood with everyone else while Holly gave us our day's assignments. A small group of folks didn't have instructions, so I approached them and asked if anyone was interested in driving to Waveland, Mississippi, to save some puppies. Two women stepped forward. One was the famous author Joyce Maynard and the other a woman traveling with her. Joyce was writing a piece for a San Francisco newspaper about the animal rescue efforts. They wanted to help. I gave them a quick primer on Waveland and dealing with the staff, directions, and a warning: get in and get out as quickly as possible. I was worried Roberta might change her mind.

A few hours later, Joyce returned with fifteen puppies, the mother dogs for the puppies, and two other dogs Roberta had relinquished. Someone set up a large circular puppy pen in the middle of the staging area, and blankets and toys with large bowls of food and water were filled to overflowing. The puppies played and slept and made us laugh out loud with their little puppy antics. Some stood on hind legs looking to be picked up, while others wrestled with one another. They were held and fawned over. The puppies were adorable and brought a respite to the suffering for all of us that evening. My relief at the sight was immeasurable. They were going to be OK. They were safe now, and all of their lives lay optimistically ahead of them.

The first few nights in New Orleans, Honey Bear and I slept in the Sequoia behind the locked gate. People were always coming and going, and some were trapping animals in the dead of night. There were always folks around. I felt safe. I'd climb on top of my sleeping bag and try to get as comfortable as possible. The nights were humid, and it was hard to keep the windows open because of the mosquitoes. I'd never seen the likes of Louisiana mosquitoes. They were like small airplanes. Honey had been diagnosed with heartworms, a mosquito-borne disease, prevalent in many southern dogs, and she had a "hotspot" on one side of her torso. She was being treated for both at the clinic around the corner. Every night I'd apply her ointment and walk her around the block before we went to bed. The two of us were inseparable.

Holly had been given the keys to an empty apartment on Coliseum Street in the Garden District. It was in a beautiful, old two-story house with an elegant entryway with gorgeous carved wooden handrails leading to the second floor. Most of the shingles had blown off of the roof, but the windows were still intact. After a few days, she invited me to stay with her and a few of the others. I jumped at the chance, and our first night, Honey and I slept in the kitchen on the floor. It was a small studio whose only drawback was a gaping hole in the ceiling that opened to the night sky beyond. One night, six of us stayed there, and we slept huddled up next to each other to get away from the falling plaster. Every night we were dead tired but still found the energy to share the day's stories. Sometimes there were tears when an incredibly sad encounter was shared. We'd all listen intently despite our own troubling tales. And everyone was patient as we took turns showering in the one small bathroom.

Our shared experiences of the tragedies we witnessed and the daunting heat and dust that made our clothes condemnable didn't matter to us. We shared our triumphs and our disappointments. We cried together, huddled in small groups when we learned of another family missing their pet or another story about what was happening in the Lower Ninth Ward. Those stories are too hard to tell here. We saw pictures none of us will ever forget, the suffering seared into our memory. We lived and breathed for each other, for another day, to save one more life.

Looking back on all of this over the years, I've tried to make sense of it. I left Massachusetts intending to do something to help what I saw as a desperate situation and a blundered response to a national emergency. I knew the animals needed help, and I thought I'd be gone for a few weeks, do what I could, and return home to my life. But pulling animals from the Waveland Animal Shelter became my obsession and my curse. It was all I could think about. I worried incessantly when I wasn't there. A few other volunteers had stumbled onto Waveland, but their visits were sporadic and unreliable. I assumed a sense of ownership for the situation and an inflated sense of responsibility for what I could realistically do from 1,600 miles away. On each subsequent trip I took to New Orleans, I would inevitably head east on the I-10 and pull as many dogs and puppies as Rob and Holly would allow. When I wasn't down south, boots on the ground, I would ask my newfound friends to go to Waveland and pull them. And every time I boarded a plane to head home, I would ask those that were staying behind to not forget the animals in Waveland, Mississippi.

The days were exhausting and exhilarating. In early November, New Orleans was still as hot as hell. Every day I'd line up with the others and get my assignments. I kept the feeding and watering stations stocked. I drove the streets looking for strays. Waveland was never far from my thoughts. Most nights before bed, I'd lie on my sleeping bag, my laptop propped against my tented legs, searching for shelters throughout the United States that were willing to take in Katrina's animal survivors.

One day on Magazine, I saw a small woman packing some serious photographic hardware. Carol Guzy was a photographer for the *Washington Post*. She had been on assignment in Texas when Katrina hit, and her editor told her to drop everything and go. A few weeks later, as the story became victim to the news cycle's short-term memory, her editor told her to return to DC. But like so many others, she couldn't leave. She pleaded with them to let her stay. There was a remarkable story in New Orleans regarding the animal rescue efforts, and she wouldn't accept no. She had to be the one to document it. They insisted she return.

A small woman with long blond hair who never went anywhere without three large cameras around her neck, she had a face that quickly changed from a broad smile to intense concentration. Possessing a remarkable eye, Carol had won four Pulitzer Prizes for her photojournalism. She had spent her career ricocheting worldwide, a journalistic first responder sent to chronicle war, famine, cataclysm, and natural disaster. She had seen Colombians buried alive by a mudslide, Haitian children crushed at their school desks in an earthquake, a man knifed to death by an angry mob in Somalia. She brought an intimacy to her work that made it impossible for anyone with a heart to look away. But her unending exposure to the suffering and inhumanity in the world hadn't hardened her at all; she was a resilient soul who would forever be burdened with emotional wounds. Carol disregarded the unspoken rule that journalists stay unbiased and uninvolved. She adopted as her godson a boy she met while photographing young amputees who had survived machete attacks by guerrillas in Sierra Leone, supporting him for years and helping put him through school. She adored animals and always had a menagerie back home of sick or injured refugees she had taken in and nursed back to health. Like so many of us who had raced to the Gulf intending to do whatever we could for a week or two and then leave, Carol had found it impossible to stay away. After her editors summoned her back home to move onto other assignments, Carol negotiated a six-month leave of absence to immerse herself in and document the animal rescue effort. "This is a story that must be told," she said to her editors.

Carol and I became good friends during my first trips to Hound Zero, and we grew close. Professional to a fault, she never got in the way while we traveled the city streets to save animals. Her camera almost always attached to her right eye; the rat-a-tat of the auto shutter was the backdrop for remarkable images. Her photos became the permanent record from which we all came to understand exactly what we had done.

If the heat and horror were not challenging enough, the stories we were hearing from rescuers in other parts of the city were distressing, to say the least. The Lower Ninth Ward and St. Bernard's Parish had been closed off to all but the military and police. Word was the local shelter had been given exclusive access to trap animals in those neighborhoods and that all that were found would be killed.

When the authorities opened the Lower Ninth and St. Bernard Parish, we caravanned out one bright, sunny day. Rob asked if I could bring traps to a parish school, where they were building a trapping supply area and a holding pen for the animals. So Barb and I loaded up our vehicle and drove through the Lower Ninth Ward to St. Bernard's.

Downtown New Orleans was deserted, and Central City was severely flooded, but the trip through the Lower Ninth and into St. Bernard's was an absolute shock. Located on the western banks of the Mississippi River Gulf Outlet Canal, the "MRGO" was a seventy-six-mile-long waterway built by the US Army Corps of Engineers in the mid-twentieth century to shorten the navigation route between the Gulf of Mexico and the Port of New Orleans. And while the actual hurricane decimated everything east of the Pearl River to the state of Alabama, the MRGO was mostly responsible for the overwhelming storm surge that devastated the greater New Orleans area. The MRGO had provided an unimpeded storm surge path into the lower-lying neighborhoods of east New Orleans. They didn't stand a chance of surviving the angry waters. The homes in this area were almost exclusively mid-twentieth century wooden structures housing tightly knit low-income Black communities. Scattered to the winds and bused throughout the United States many could not return.

Nothing could have prepared us for what we saw in the eastern parishes. It was a police state. Every major road leading into St. Bernard's had military checkpoints. Helicopters hovered above us. If you were not a resident or a relief worker, you didn't get in. If you did get in, you got out by dark. There was a curfew.

We had a cargo van and two SUVs. Driving down the main thoroughfare, we saw two dogs running scared across the road. One was a small dachshund and the other a large black Lab-type dog. We pulled over, and four of our team jumped out and went after them. We had stopped in front of a boarded-up one-story brick house, and a man was wildly waving his arms and pointing to the running dogs. While the others began their pursuit, I went to meet him. He started talking in a strong, nearly undecipherable south Louisiana Cajun accent. He told me his name was Gary. He was thin and sunburnt, a dirty baseball cap held back stringy, long blonde hair. I tried to make out what he was saying as he pointed to a nearby shuttered shack. It took a minute for me to understand. He was telling me a cat was hiding underneath the shack. I began walking towards the shack when he stopped me and explained it was his cat, and she wouldn't come to him. I looked out on the road to see where my friends were. The dogs had turned down a side street, and they were still in pursuit. I felt a hand on my shoulder, and I turned around. Gary wrapped both arms around me, put his head on my shoulder, and started to cry. I held him, and through his sobs, I understood that four of his cats had drowned in the flood. This cat was the only one he had left. And this cat no longer knew who he was.

He pointed out his house to me. It was the boarded-up brick house we had been standing in front of. Its large yard was parched and dry, the bushes framing the doorway brown and brittle. Gary took my hand, and we walked around back.

He had placed food, water, and a small litter box outside for his kitty. It was under the overhang that provided a small amount of shade from the ever-present sun. He turned and pointed to a small raised mound of dirt that had a solitary, little, plastic red rose sticking out of its middle. Through his tears, I understood it was where he had buried his cats. Something broke in my chest. I turned and walked towards the small house. His cat was sitting on the little stoop out front, but she ran under the crawlspace as we got closer.

The house was on small stilts like most homes in the parish, and the crawl space made it challenging for rescue. I knew I'd need more help to get Gary's cat. Marilyn was an experienced trapper, and she was one of the folks that had gone after the two dogs. A native New Orleanian who had rescued many animals before the storm, she and her husband lost their home. Her husband, their nine dogs, and many cats lived in a trailer where their house once stood. They didn't have electricity or running water. Every day she worked at Magazine. The first time I met her, she told me there was no time to think about what they had lost.

The team had been gone about ten minutes when I watched them walk back to the vehicles. They looked dejected, their catchpoles sadly by their sides. I told Marilyn about Gary's cat. I wanted nothing more than to catch Gary's cat. Marilyn went over and got down on her knees to peer under the shack. She'd need to set a trap, she told me. We didn't have smaller traps with us, so she promised him she would set a trap the next day. I held both of his arms as I tried my best to assure him we would be back for his cat. His eyes glistened from the tears, and a small smile creased his face. When I turned and walked away, my eyes began to sting and burn. Tears welled and streamed down my face. I felt myself choke back a sob. The sadness overwhelmed and consumed me. The countless vulnerable faces and the sadness of an entire city. The people like Gary, who never meant for their animals to be harmed. Never for a moment thought they'd be gone for so long. My own levee breached; I couldn't hold back my tears in anymore.

That was my last full day in New Orleans, my first trip. My own dogs were being cared for by friends, and the emotional exhaustion was beginning to take its toll. I wouldn't be back the next day to help catch Gary's cat, and that was the thing that made me saddest of all. But Honey needed to be in a home to begin the recovery from her heartworm treatment, and the hotspot on her side required care. I knew I had to get us home. The small border collie mix that Barb was concerned about was languishing in Waveland. She told me often that she couldn't get him off of her mind. I promised her I'd pick him up on my way back home. Fortunately, a couple in Pennsylvania had spent time in New Orleans with Althea, and they wanted me to drop him off with them. Reluctantly I packed my gear and said my goodbyes. I felt guilty leaving my friends behind. What if others didn't show? What if the access extended us was suddenly denied, and we could no longer find the animals? It was mid-November 2005, and for the rest of the country, Katrina was over. Who would come in behind me and take up the slack? And what about Waveland? In twelve short days, I had experienced something profound, and letting it go felt impossible. Reluctantly I climbed up into the Sequoia for the long ride to Massachusetts. Honey was riding shotgun on a bed of blankets, and we had one more stop to make.

An hour outside of New Orleans and the early morning sun looked smoky white, like a hot piece of cotton in the sky. The air felt slick and wet with heat; the road ahead was long. The I-10 outside Slidell, Louisiana, was lined with car dealerships closed since August 29. The cars were still lined up facing the highway, every single one of them soot-covered gray.

I pulled into Waveland about 10:00 a.m., my SUV kicking up a dust storm in its wake. It had rained little since the hurricane, and the earth was dying of thirst, the ground hard and crusty. One of the animal control officers came outside and pulled me aside. He told me there was a dog that had been brought in the night prior. He'd been hit by a car, and they thought his back was broken. I asked where the dog was and walked as fast as I could to the first run in the shelter's outdoor area. I looked through the gate and saw a small black dog lying on its side with just a flimsy towel under his body. His breathing was fast due to the heat and the pain. His brown eyes looked up at me.

Roberta and Tori came through the door to see what I was up to. When I asked Roberta what she was going to do about the dog, she replied, "Nothing." I opened the gate to his cage. "He's suffering, Roberta, you can't just leave him here." She looked down at him, then over at me, and with a blank expression, she replied, "Suffering? That dog ain't sufferin.'"

I felt sick. Enraged. The apathy, cruelty, and sadness surrounding me for days, and now the one person paid to care for these animals was just going to let them suffer. There was nothing I could do. I turned to walk away. I wanted to hurt her. I wanted to hurt her bad. Instead, I kept walking. I walked because if I said anything more or tried to take the dog with me, I would jeopardize the volunteer's fragile relationship with the shelter. I'd give them the one reason they were looking for to bar the rescue community. I walked around the city shed next door, out of sight of the shelter. I clenched my fists and swore, tears stinging my eyes. Chubby, the animal control officer, had followed me. "There's nothing you can do," he said. "Roberta doesn't care about no animals, and she's sure not gonna let you do nothing about it. Jus' get on your way."

He asked me to follow him to his truck. In the back was a cardboard box with four pit bull puppies in it. He told me I should take them because the staff couldn't adopt out pits and they'd just be put down. The poor things were all huddled in a corner, scared to death, their breathing labored in the beating sun. They were just babies. He told me to pull the Sequoia up to his truck so he could put them inside.

I walked back to the shelter, wiping tears from my eyes, and went to the run where Barb's border collie was. I promised her I wouldn't leave him in there, and I didn't. Holly and Rob gave me a few crates when I left New Orleans, and I loaded him in one. A pair of bonded dogs had been brought in a few days prior, and I took them too. They could travel in one crate. The four puppies fit in another large crate. There was no more room.

When I left Cape Cod in late October, I had no understanding of what I would find when I arrived on the stricken Gulf Coast. Armed with so little, I figured out the next step by walking into the unknown. My body weary and my heart heavy, I let my mind wander back to all I had done. The feelings of elation and relief every time we found animals still alive. The anticipation and fear when we were able to trap a scared dog. The joy when we watched them drink and eat and gradually lie down. The first time they let us pet their dirty, matted fur. The camaraderie in the human chain of loving hands loading up the Best Friends truck every night. Each of us knowing that these animals were the lucky ones. They were getting out of there. And the sadness. The dead animals we found. Some still with collars around their necks. A beloved pet. The sick ones that had suffered through weeks of starvation and dehydration. The infected eyes, the burned pads, the feral animals that had forgotten or never knew love, and were now scared to death of humans. The animals left behind to die and the pain of the people who had no idea they were leaving for a long time.

I headed north towards Atlanta, tears flooding my eyes. The puppies whimpered for a while and then grew still. Honey napped on the seat beside me. I called a local Mississippi woman from In Defense of Animals and told her about the broken dog suffering in Waveland. She told me she'd go get him. The staff was more likely to surrender him to one of their own. Outside Atlanta, the daylight well behind me, I headed east on I-285 to avoid downtown. Fatigue had set in. As the miles passed, scenes kept flashing through my mind: The dead dogs on the sides of roads. The disgusting and decaying smell of the refrigerators, and the soldiers with their guns. Drinking café au lait with newfound friends during a brief break in the French Quarter, the feeling like I had done something, made something of my life. The images of homemade graves in barren backyards and the spray-painted homes left to rot in the swollen sun, their people long gone, or worse. The sadness of my time in the south caught up with and ran over me like a fast-moving train. I couldn't read the interstate signs. My eyes opened and flooded like the streets I'd walked through, and I couldn't find my way off the interstate. I couldn't think. I couldn't see. I kept circling and circling Atlanta.

I had to stop. I had to sleep. But I had eight dogs with me, and where would I find a place that would take us? I called a friend back home and asked her to find a hotel between Atlanta and Charlotte, North Carolina. She told me to give her ten minutes. It felt like the longest ten minutes of my life, but the phone rang, and there she was—a Marriot in Spartanburg, South Carolina, would take us in. But it was still 175 miles away. I had to get my head together if I was going to make it. I had to find my way off the road.

At 2:00 a.m., I pulled into the Marriot parking lot. Two young guys were hanging around the office, and I asked them if they would help me with the dogs. They jumped at the opportunity. We carried the crates with the puppies, Henry the border collie, and the two bonded mutts into the room. Honey walked on her leash. I thanked the guys profusely and started getting the animals settled in. The poor puppies were covered in fleas. I carried them into the bathroom and put them in the tub. They were terrified of me and shook furiously. What the hell was I going to do? I didn't have a flea comb or powder, and the poor things were infested. If I didn't do something, they would continue to suffer. I bathed them with the complimentary shampoo and toweled them off as best I could. The dirty water with dead fleas was circling the drain. At least I got some of them. The pups would have to stay in the bathroom all night.

Henry and the bonded pair were fast asleep in their crates, and Honey Bear, who I had put up on the bed, was curled up in a ball. Her soft, reddish fur moved with each breath. I turned off the lights, fully dressed, and fell into a deep, dark sleep on top of the comforter, my body too weak to cover. Four hours later, the sun streaming in the window, I awoke, loaded up, and headed home.

By the time I got back to Cape Cod, it was very late on a Friday night. The puppies and the bonded pair were dropped off at a sanctuary in North Carolina that I had found online and had prearranged for their placement. Henry was delivered to the couple in Pennsylvania. It was just Honey and me. Home.

I stayed for two days.

Stranded on an overpass for the I-10, New Orleans.

Early efforts by the military, New Orleans.

The helplessness and despair of the New Orleans Superdome.

Beware.

Desperate measures in a desperate situation.

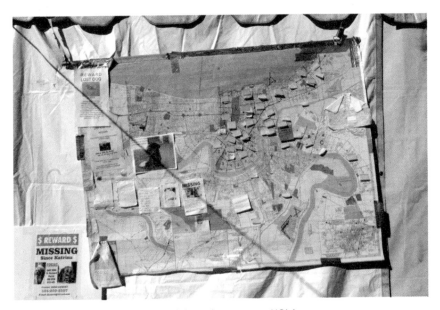

Tracking the rescue teams dispersed throughout greater NOLA.

Saving an abandoned dog in a devasted home in the Lower Ninth Ward.

Looking for animals in homes that flooded.

Conditions in most homes were very dangerous with minimal protection.

Sarah Rose saving a newborn puppy underneath a New Orleans home.

At times the magnitude of the suffering was paralyzing.

Saving a litter of newborn puppies.

Making every effort to save cats and kittens from a soon to be razed park in Kenner.

Underneath a NOLA home.

Reunions were few, but kept the rescuers committed and hopeful.

An elderly resident finds her dog.

A NOLA resident the moment she realizes her beloved parrot was saved.

Relief. Gratitude. Love.

It was dangerous. But no one gave their safety a second thought. We had to save the animals.

Trixie and Chris McLaughlin, Celebration Station, New Orleans. February 2006.

Carol Guzy and Trixie. Celebration Station, New Orleans.

Carol and Trixie in a rare quiet moment.

A kitten in the arms of an angel.

Chapter Four

Home

A glacial moraine only twenty miles wide at its girth "the Cape," as the locals refer to it, is a fragile ecological environment and is home to many endangered migrating species. It is a magical place to live or visit, and when Katrina struck the Gulf Coast in late August of 2005, it was the place I called home. Since early June, I had lived in Wellfleet and Truro, and it was on a Truro bayside beach that I first fielded calls from Jerry, Lisa, Kim, and Catherine—all people I had never met, but they had received my desperate email pleas for help.

The four of them were ready to roll.

But roll to where?

For ten days, my sister had been calling me from New Orleans. Althea, a lifelong animal lover, had self-deployed. She had read many reports online about where to go and who needed help. She made a list of the makeshift rescue centers that had sprung up around the city and decided where to go.

Flying into New Orleans was not possible, so she booked a flight to Baton Rouge, rented a car and headed to the Lamar Dixon Expo Center. The Humane Society of the United States, LSU Veterinary School, the International Fund for Animal

Welfare, and others had set up an emergency shelter at Lamar Dixon in Gonzales, Louisiana. Animals that were left in the city were brought there in the hopes of reuniting them with their families. It was mid-September, and animal lovers from all over the US had volunteered to go to New Orleans. Althea found lists online of what to bring to a disaster zone, but they proved to be inadequate for addressing the needs of animal rescuers. There were no lists for that category.

She notified her employer that she had to take some personal time and armed with little more than clothes, a flashlight, and money a few friends had donated, she got on a plane to Louisiana. When she arrived, she was one of the people who went door-to-door in New Orleans, checking to see if any animals were still alive inside. For known addresses where animals had been reported, they busted down doors or through windows. In the first home my sister entered, she found a dead collie in the living room. It was heartbreaking work.

In mid-September, the city was still flooded, the airport struggling to reopen. Every night she'd call and tell me about her day. After our calls, I'd write everything down in an email and send it to our extended group of friends who wanted to know what was happening to the animals.

A strict curfew was in force. The animal rescuers had to vacate the city by 6:00 p.m., or they risked being shot by the military. Tensions ran very high with memories of what happened at the Superdome, not far from anyone's mind. The violence after days of folks sweltering in the building with no water or food. Looting and a depleted police force made a deadly combination and chaos ensued. To say her stories were disturbing is a gross understatement. One night she got stuck in New Orleans after curfew. They had lost track of time and she found herself in the French Quarter. Some of the bars were open and there were a few hotels that had rooms for rent. As we talked, she suddenly interrupted me: "Shit, shit!" she said. "The police are behind us and their blue lights are flashing. I've got to go!"

Click.

The New Orleans Police Department had been disparaged by every news outlet since the storm. The force was severely depleted when some of the officers took their families and evacuated. Looting and crime ensued. The police who stayed had the monumental task of restoring order in a city that had been plundered and vandalized. And now my sister had been pulled over after curfew. I waited and waited for what felt like an impossibly long time. My mind created every adverse scenario it could. They'd get arrested and brought in for trespassing. They'd be mistaken for criminals and shot. I waited and waited. My phone didn't ring.

Finally, I gave into my building terror, and I called her back. She answered the phone in a light and playful manner. "What the hell happened?" I asked. "What? Ohhhh, *that!*" she said. "They had bottle baby kittens in the back seat of their cruiser. They wanted to know if we had any kitten formula." My fear melted into relief with a straight shot of warmth at the thought of the police caring for bottle baby kittens. During another call we laughed hysterically when she called to tell me she had fleas. But the lighter stories were far outnumbered.

Of all the horror stories, the one that was the hardest was the day a woman showed up at Lamar Dixon to complete a missing animal report. In the margins of the page, she wrote, "My son committed suicide after the hurricane. I just have to find his dogs." One of Althea's peers said she walked the woman through the holding areas, and all she did was cry.

The more Althea told me, the more I feared for her life. Every day she awoke and put herself in harm's way by driving in a city where many residents were not allowed and by breaking down doors, not knowing what awaited on the other side. By late September, the people of New Orleans were growing more desperate with each passing day. There was little to no infrastructure, and sheltering situations were overcrowded and lacking in basic necessities. Families had been torn apart. Neighbors had drowned in their attics.

One morning my sister called, and she sounded particularly distraught. "This morning, the coordinators told us there was a database of six thousand addresses for homes where animals had been left behind. Can you please send out an email and ask for help?" That morning the animal rescue effort at Lamar Dixon had one hundred volunteers. And time was running out.

Althea's organizational skills were coveted, and after a few days in New Orleans, she was reassigned to coordinating the volunteer and reunification effort. She told me of a guy in his twenties who showed up at Lamar Dixon looking for his pet reptile. He was searching the pet holding area when suddenly people heard screaming and everyone wondered what the hell was going on. In a cage was his, well . . . she really didn't know what it was, but it was his pet, his best friend, and there she was all safe and sound. He couldn't believe the kindness of strangers traveling from all over to save the one thing he thought he had lost forever. Over and over, people would tell us how amazed they were that we walked away from our lives to try to help theirs. One person asked my sister for her mailing address. "When this is all over," he said, "I know my wife will want to send you a thank you card."

Her time at Lamar Dixon was gratifying, but she found that being away from the city and not actively searching for animals had left her with a case of survivor guilt. She asked to be sent back into the city. On a particularly gorgeous sunny day, she drove the streets of Gentilly. I was on the phone with her as she read me the street names—Wisteria, Sage, Spain, Art, Vienna, and Jasmine. All that was pretty about them now were their names. It was that day she said to me, "the only thing worse than what's on the outside is what's on the inside."

Massachusetts and Mississippi are as opposite in culture and climate as one can experience in the continental United States. Politically and socially, they could not be more disparate.

In late August 2005, Massachusetts's weather was on its way to the annual transition to fall, while Mississippi's average temperatures were still in the low nineties. By October, when I first arrived, the daytime temps were still warm enough for swimming, but back home, the leaves had made their way from bright red and orange to yellow and brown.

On opposite ends of the educational spectrum, Mississippians generally see northerners as "book smart," which is a put-down. We're emotionally cold, and it would be best if we'd mind our own business. Their southern sweetness is thick, and they dispense it with ease, but they're fiercely independent and proud of their southern traditions. Religion reigns supreme. Outsiders, and that can mean folks from the next county, never mind from a blue state north of the Mason-Dixon, aren't always welcome. I experienced examples of this attitude over and over again.

When I went to Mississippi, I felt like I was in another country. The weather felt welcoming, but most folks did not. I was an "outsider," I quickly learned, and a "Yankee," to make matters just about as bad as they could be.

In New Orleans, it was much different. Most welcomed the animal rescue first responders. In the immediate area surrounding our makeshift headquarters, a few people still lived in their rain-soaked apartments and homes and on sweltering late summer nights when the cicadas created a sound like the cacophony of a siren screaming, they would walk their dogs down the abandoned streets. One day, an older man stopped me on a side street by a water pumping station. He approached my vehicle and handed me a $100 bill. I adamantly refused it, but he insisted. "Y'all are doing good," he said. "Please, take it." I used it for Honey Bear's vet bill.

Being home was a shock. Early winter had arrived, and there was a cold blue chill in the breeze. It was dreary on Cape Cod, my first morning home, the skies darkened and aluminum gray. I awoke disoriented and downcast. My body hurt. My heart hurt. All I could think about was what my friends were doing right then. How many animals had they found dead or dying last night? How many volunteers had shown up to help? Were there enough hands to load the animals onto the Best Friends truck and who was filling the feeding stations I had come to personally know?

I had grown up in an extended family that had a long tradition of military service. My paternal grandparents both came from huge families, and my great aunts and uncles were a consistent and loving presence in my early years. My grandfather's four brothers fought in World War II, and when the Japanese attacked Pearl Harbor, two great uncles were deployed there.

On my mom's side, my grandfather enlisted in the US Navy and served in the Pacific Theatre. He received a Purple Heart for his service.

My dad and his brother were the last generation to serve, Dad in the navy and my uncle John, the army. I have not been to war. But I imagined it looked something like the Gulf Coast of the United States after Hurricane Katrina. Our motley crew of animal lovers may not have been trained to serve on the frontlines of a battlefield, but in many ways, that is precisely what we were doing. It was a race against time for the animals. We banded together, improvised, and no one suffered alone. Even the exhaustion of having spent many hours tracking dogs, walking neighborhoods in the intense heat and humidity, loading up panel trucks, and having our hearts broken when we got there just a little too late, didn't shake our resolve. Even then, no one stopped working or trying. Relationships were made and broken. The emotional toll of time away from home or a significant other who didn't understand the calling led some to form relationships while others sought out divorce. For me, that meant returning over and over again.

I made coffee. No one was home. I was glad to be alone, so I wouldn't have to talk. Honey was in a crate in the bedroom, and she peered out at me with soft eyes. I wrapped a loose lead around her neck and slowly brought her downstairs to take her outside. Macy and Demi followed. Honey's first injection for heartworm disease had been given in New Orleans, and I had strict instructions not to let her get too excited or walk for very long. Running loose was forbidden. Her heart had to stay calm.

When we came back inside, I sat down at the kitchen table. My friends in New Orleans were waking up without running water. They were waking up dirty and tired. Some were waking up depressed and overwhelmed; the task at hand daunting. The day ahead an unknown. Others were taking inventory of the meager supplies and wondering how they would continue to care for the storm's forgotten.

I drank my coffee. It was an effort. The questions kept banging around in my head, and I felt overcome with guilt. I was sitting in the kitchen of a beautiful Cape Cod home, in a comfortable chair, with a decent cup of coffee.

What was I doing here?

Alone, my friends out at work all day I stayed close to home and slept, my body a dead weight, a burden no longer belonging to me. The only reason to get out of bed was to take care of the dogs.

By Sunday, I felt a little less tired. The day broke bright and cool. Summer cottages were boarded up, and the roads were less busy. Shops displayed their "closed for the season" and "see you in the spring" signs, and I was already thinking about returning to New Orleans. I had to go back. Eastern Mountain Sports in Hyannis was discounting gear for Katrina first responders. With the knowledge I had gained by being on the ground for twelve days, I knew better now what I would need to survive. And this time I would fly down so I'd be without a vehicle to sleep in. I'd need a sleeping bag and a small pillow. A headlamp for seeing under houses and buildings was a luxury and a necessity. This would free my hands to grab the dogs. I headed to Hyannis.

The falling, dead leaves danced in the chilly breeze. The trees still standing and the homes with shingled roofs were a sharp contrast to the world I have just left. There was little traffic on Cape Cod in November but much more than I had seen on the Gulf Coast. It didn't feel real. It didn't feel right. So much devastation and sorrow had surrounded me for two weeks. I felt like an interloper, a stranger in my own land. I no longer belonged where I was. I drove in silence, my thoughts swirling like the leaves.

In Hyannis I found a decent sleeping bag and a compressible pillow. A friend had bought me a military jumpsuit from the local army/navy surplus store, and I purchased a pair of Merrell boots to complete my wardrobe. The boots would last one trip. They'd have to be disposed of before I came home. I didn't want to bring back what I'd be walking through. A headlamp filled out my gear. I paid with a credit card and headed home.

The mall was a mile up the road, so I decided to stop for a quick lunch. The food court was filled with people. I sat at a table alone. Carnival music played loudly in the distance as the small carousel in the food court of the Cape Cod Mall went 'round and 'round. It was loaded up with small children sitting on painted and pretty, brightly colored wooden horses. The world had kept spinning. The night became day, and days turned into weeks, but for New Orleans and Mississippi, the world had stopped. It was mired in mud and misery, and the schools were choked with weeds. The horses were dead, locked, and drowned in their stalls; their rotting flesh and bleached white bones all that remained. But, on this day in mid-November 2005, the horses were painted in bright colors. The shoppers stopped and watched the children laugh and play. But the children of New Orleans were not playing. And the dogs were dying.

I watched the brightly painted horses move up and down, and the little chariots were filled. I looked down at my food, but my appetite was suddenly gone. I looked around. Mothers were tending to their children, and couples looked deep in conversation. Workers were grabbing a quick bite to eat, and that carousel kept going 'round and 'round. It was loud. It was getting louder and louder as I watched a young couple at the next table with their two kids. It all seemed so normal. But there was no normal for me anymore. And there certainly was no normal for the folks on the Gulf Coast.

As my thoughts darkened, the chatter increased until all I could hear was one loud crescendo of noise. I felt like I was falling into a deep, dark tunnel, spiraling down into the darkness. My thoughts flashed to the car ride there. The highway on both sides lined with trees. The trees were standing. And the houses and buildings were perfect, not a single shutter or shingle out of place. The roads were clear of debris, and the stoplights worked.

The animals were safe.

Nothing made sense anymore. My thoughts continued to spiral, and the noise increased in my ears. I felt a sudden urge to stand on my table and yell, "Do you people have any idea what is going on in your own country? New Orleans and the Gulf Coast of Mississippi are *gone*, goddammit, and all of you are acting like nothing has happened! The animals are *dying*! The place is a wasteland. The people are scattered and homeless, and you don't have a fucking clue!"

The reality of my experience had made its own personal landfall. I threw my uneaten food in a barrel. I drove home in a hurry knowing precisely what I had to do. I told my roommates I needed their help caring for Honey, and my dogs and I booked a flight.

Twenty-four hours later, I boarded a plane to New Orleans.

Chapter Five

Hound Zero

The flight from Atlanta to New Orleans was short, and the plane was small. The woman in my row did not acknowledge me when I sat down. I threw my carry-on bag under the seat in front of me and anxiously awaited our landing. I couldn't wait to hit the ground.

I was nervous, jumpy, and I couldn't concentrate to read. What would this trip bring? How many animals had my friends been able to save? How many people were still wandering the streets looking for their own? I wanted to talk to someone, get my mind off things. I needed to reach out to someone who had seen the city and felt the pain. Someone who understood and spoke the same language. The language of destruction and despair. It was impossible to articulate all I had seen and done to the people in my life pre-Katrina. Home no longer felt like home. Home was where my friends and the animals were. Home was New Orleans and southern Mississippi.

A few times, my eyes glanced at the woman in the seat next to me, but she just stared out the window, her long hair covering her eyes. I sensed she wanted to be left alone. I flipped through a magazine and glanced around the cabin.

Halfway through the flight, the pilot announced we were beginning our initial approach to New Orleans. His words seemed to bring her back from her reverie. She looked around the cabin and then to no one, in particular, said, "Why are these people going to New Orleans? There's nothing there."

An awkward moment passed while I waited for her to say something else. The quiet grew between us. I asked her if she was from New Orleans. And it was as if a levee had burst within her. For the next twenty-five minutes, she talked nonstop.

Her name was Amy, and she lived in Lakeview. I knew from my first trip that the failure of the Seventeenth Street levee had completely flooded Lakeview. It was where Ted and Judy Goncalves lived. Amy worked for the Ritz-Carlton downtown, and when Tropical Storm 12 burst into Hurricane Katrina, she decided to evacuate there. She mistakenly believed she'd be safe in a building of mortar and brick, standing forty stories high.

She wasn't the only local who made that mistake. Many who had the means to leave, but decided against it, evacuated to the hotels. Adventure-ready tourists mistakenly stayed as well. The hotels in New Orleans filled quickly. Many became evacuation centers. Amy hunkered down in a room with five New Orleans police officers, one or two of whom were friends. Guys she knew before their world busted apart and washed away. They occupied a suite on one of the upper floors and watched the city below toss in the wind. For two days, the wind thrashed at the windows and the building swayed, but they stayed relatively safe high above New Orleans's Central Business District, or CBD, as the locals know it. It was there they watched the dark water rise.

Within a few days, they were running out of food and water. The occupancy of the hotel had swelled to 1,600 people, and tempers began to flare. By the fifth day, they started hearing stories that the situation at the Superdome had deteriorated, and the folks there were desperate and threatening to take over the hotels. Amy and her friends decided they had to leave. They got their few belongings together and started down the stairs. The elevators did not work. When they got to the lobby, it was chaos. They headed for the doors but were quickly warned that they couldn't go outside. Someone was shooting at anyone who tried to leave the hotel. One of her friends gave her a loaded gun. They decided to head back up to their room.

The next day they tried again to leave the hotel. One of the guys snuck out the back through the loading dock and flagged a military truck patrolling adjacent streets. The soldiers were persuaded to help them evacuate, and they pulled into the loading dock of the hotel, and while soldiers surrounded the truck, they fired warning shots into the air. Amy and her friends climbed in the back.

While she told me her story, she betrayed little emotion. Her eyes held the same vacant stare, and her words were soft and eerily distant, like they belonged to someone else, like it wasn't her story she was telling. Erroneous reports circulated, and it was hard to tell fact from fiction. But Amy was living proof, and she was sitting right next to me. This woman had lived in New Orleans her whole life. She had a nice job at the Ritz, and she owned a home in Lakeview, an upper-middle-class, predominately white neighborhood. She lived the American dream, and in one day, her life was reduced to carrying a gun and being in a shootout to survive in the middle of her major, metropolitan all-American city.

Her parents, sisters, and brothers all lived in New Orleans too. Every single one of their homes was lost to the levee failures. All I could do was sit and listen. She finished her story as we began the descent into New Orleans. Losing her house and everything she owned was terrible, but that wasn't the hardest part for her. Nor was the fact that she had to carry a gun to survive for a few days, holed up in a five-star hotel. Her hometown was drowning, and her neighbors were taking to the roofs with guns, shooting at each other, but that wasn't the worst part. The part that was hardest, the thing that finally opened her eyes and spilled her tears, was when she talked of her parents and their home in Chalmette, the home where she grew up. The place where Gary lived too. All the pictures, all the memories, she said, "are all gone now."

We disembarked together, and I wished her well. I didn't know what else to say. I headed to the rental car station, rented the largest vehicle they had, grabbed my checked bag, and headed to Magazine. I pulled into a full parking lot and was relieved to see so much activity. People were walking dogs, filling out paperwork, loading up vans with food and water, generally keeping very busy. A mountain rescue team from Washington State wore bright red shirts, and somehow Rob had gotten a bunch of blue shirts with yellow lettering that read, "Animal Rescue." They were in the back of his pickup, and he handed them out to us all. We wore them with pride.

I couldn't wait to hit the streets.

Alvin Bean, a rescuer from Virginia, was loading up the Budget cargo van and getting ready to do some tracking in Lakeview. I asked her if I could go along. In less than an hour, I'd be back on the streets.

Alvin had been in New Orleans since the first floods came. At 5' 6", with long brown hair tied in a long pigtail that snaked down her back, it was her skill as a tracker that made her so valuable to the rescue efforts. And the thick layers of mud and silt made for perfect conditions for tracking tiny paw prints.

It was my first rescue trip to Lakeview. The same neighborhood my seatmate on the plane, Amy, had lived but was no longer allowed in. Less than two hours after meeting her, I was driving through Lakeview, wondering which house was hers.

The ride to Lakeview took fifteen minutes due west on the I-10. Exiting the interstate, we drove a few minutes and turned right onto a road that had large construction horses with signs attached warning us not to enter unless we were "authorized personnel." Sometimes we were, and sometimes we weren't. It seemed to depend on who stopped us. We proceeded, hoping if we were stopped, we wouldn't get arrested for trespassing.

Most of the houses were still standing, the red brick ones having fared significantly better than their wooden counterparts. Every single one had the spray-painted mark of Katrina—the large orange "X" or "Katrina cross," with notes in each sector identifying the search team that had left the mark, the date of the search, and how many alive or dead humans or animals had been found. Some houses had long, spray-painted notes on them describing what the rescuers wanted to convey to others. "Two cats under porch" was one. Those messages rarely conveyed anything good.

Most of the homes were two-story, and the first and second floors looked like they didn't belong to one another. The first floor had shattered windows, and the exterior was thick with mold and mud. The second floor looked relatively intact. And on every house, about twelve feet from the ground, was the high-water mark.

Alvin and I drove a long time, and every street looked the same. Large warning signs shouting, "DO NOT ENTER" or "CAUTION," were on some homes; on others were signs saying, "LOOTERS WILL BE SHOT!" Except for NOPD cruisers and construction trucks, we were the only ones in Lakeview that day. Cars were flung upside down against trees, and a boat had washed ashore in someone's front yard. On another street, we saw a boat upside down on a car as we maneuvered and bounced down the streets of Lakeview.

After driving for a while, Alvin pulled over where she had set a trap the night before. We walked around back, peeling back a piece of broken fence to access the rear. In the shade of the back patio, we saw the trap she had set. The food was still there. The trap was empty.

Alvin walked the yard in small circles studying the settled silt. The tracks she had seen that first day that had led her to this yard were partially filled now. No new tracks could be found. She thought on this hard for a minute, her face serious, her eyes squinting at the silt as if she were trying to read an unfamiliar word in a book, and then told me the animal might have moved on to another yard. She decided we'd leave the trap for one more day, and we replaced the now-rotting food that had spoiled in the heat.

We got back to Magazine in the late afternoon, and as soon as I got out of the van, Cadi ran up to me. "We couldn't wait for you to get back," she said. "There's someone here who's been looking for you." I followed her into the triage area, and there was Marilyn, down on her knees playing with a puppy.

Marilyn turned around and stood up, her face breaking into a wide smile. "I trapped Gary's cat," she said. "Min-min is back with him." I was so happy I cried while I hugged her. She had gone back the next day and set the trap like she said she would. Marilyn kept a close watch on that trap. It only took a few hours for Marilyn to catch Min-Min. I'd never see Gary again, but I'd think about him every day. I'd imagine him holding onto the one last thing he had left in this world, Min-Min. I'd hope it'd be enough to help him pull through.

I was ecstatic to be back. I felt at home, with my people, doing something meaningful and selfless. Breathing was easier, and I worried less. It didn't matter I had nowhere to sleep; none of us did. There were burritos down the street and some good coffee nearby. I'd be OK. We'd be OK. There were new people to meet, friends to make, and animals to save. I hadn't made any progress finding Manual's dog, Missy, but I knew I had to go see him. I drove out to where he had been working on his friend's home. He was so happy to see me; I hated to tell him my continued search hadn't turned up anything new. I tried to cheer him up as best as I could, and the fact that someone had photographed Missy and given her an identification number indicated to me that she was safe somewhere. I didn't feel like I was lying when I told him that.

The fifteen puppies Roberta had threatened to kill had started to get adopted. There was a small wine shop on Magazine called Sip, which had just reopened. The owner was an animal lover, and she adopted one of the Waveland pups. A young professional couple who lost their home in Lakeview had rented a second-floor apartment across the street from us. They used to sit out on their balcony at night and sip beer and watch us work. One night they decided to visit us and see what we had been up to, and they eventually ended up adopting two of the pups, naming them Katrina and Rita. They told us they wanted something positive to come out of their experience. They were the folks who coined us "Hound Zero." All of us got a real kick out of that.

I noticed that many of my rescue friends were festively adorned this trip. Mardi Gras beads in colorful clumps fell from their necks and beads in bunches of all shapes, sizes, and colors hung from rearview mirrors. I wanted some beads bad. Someone gave me the address of a Mardi Gras bead company that had tossed its inventory in their parking lot to swelter and fade in the sun. A few of us hopped in my SUV and headed to the treasure trove. When we got there, we saw a giant mountain of twisted and shining color. I'm 5' 8", and the stack was taller than I was. Man, we had a blast as we burrowed through that pile. Most strands seemed fine, their colors bright and bearing little indication they had been contaminated by the floodwaters. We loaded them up to decorate our necks and vehicles.

Rob and Holly continued to get reports of missing or abandoned pets. And many days, evacuees who had come back would flag us down on the streets. I met a family of three one day near one of the schools in Central City. Three women—a grandmother, mother, and daughter—searching for their dog. It was all I could do to listen to their story and take down their address and the description of their missing pet. The mother was the most outspoken while her daughter looked to the ground kicking around the dirt. The grandmother kept brushing away tears. They'd suffered so much and lost everything. I wanted to leave them hope. I wanted them to know we cared. I hugged them before I left and they thanked me for coming to their city. And while we didn't, couldn't, save them all, we did save many precious souls.

Some of those souls were our own.

The Lower Garden District, where Hound Zero operated, saw a strong military presence. Many patrolled in small groups, their rifles held across their chests, the barrels pointed to the sky. At Hound Zero, the soldiers walked by day and night. Since early

September, the streets of New Orleans had been crawling with brownish-green jeeps, topped with heavy canvas that flapped in the wind. Soldiers crowded their insides, their rifles by their sides, and while we were not afraid of getting arrested, mistakenly getting shot in the dark was a concern.

The Garden District of New Orleans didn't drown. Its proximity to the banks of the Mississippi River, north of the levees, kept it dry on higher ground. But there was wind damage everywhere. Windows of stately homes were covered with boards, and broken branches and downed trees littered yards and roads. Some of the homes were inhabited. They were the ones with spray-painted messages warning potential looters they'll be "shot on sight." Some of them were rented to the newly displaced from less fortunate parts of the city. The rents had shot up since the storm. For some New Orleans residents, the disaster created opportunities.

Chapter Six

Dogbusters

Rachel's underneath the shotgun shack in the Seventh Ward. She's crawling through the mud into the places no one sees: the underbellies of houses where the trash collects, the rats run, and the places where dogs hide. Her brown leather boots kick frantically, and large splotches of mud fly. We lose sight of her as she crawls inside.

Rachel's yells and the dog's growls escape through the opening where Chuck and I ripped up the floorboards and tossed them into a room that was washed and spun dry by Katrina. Out back, a videographer from the Associated Press is glued to his camera, angling for the best shot of Rachel's legs thrashing in the mud, the result of a late afternoon deluge that rained down on New Orleans. He is quiet and diligent as he goes about his business, his wide-brimmed hat dripping rain.

Rachel is barking instructions to us. We've surrounded the house and are unraveling the orange netting we took off the streets of New Orleans. We steal the bright orange roadside netting to trap the dogs because it is useless in this city of no vehicles. It helps us contain them under the crawlspaces of homes.

We are Rachel, Chuck, Laura, Cadi, Kristen, Troy, and me. We traveled from Pennsylvania, Tennessee, Canada, Florida, Connecticut, and Massachusetts. We aren't brave or courageous. We are fearless. We love animals—most of us, more than people. We tracked the dogs to this Seventh Ward shotgun and surrounded the place like a swat team. We were amateurs. We honed our skills on the fly. There had never before been a "Katrina," so there was no precedent for rescuing trapped and abandoned animals in a flooded US city. It was November, three months post-Katrina, and the dogs hadn't heard a kind word in a very long time. They had been surviving the streets of an abandoned and dying American city since August 29. They were desperate. The braver ones snarled like they'd kill us if we got any closer. We got closer anyway. One of us would crawl in after them. Small white painter's masks covered our noses and mouths, the kind they sell at hardware stores. Beat-up pairs of gardener's gloves were worn on our hands. The mask was to protect against the bacteria, stench, and death of a city rotting in a cesspool of disease. The gloves were for protection against dog bites, cuts, and dirt. We didn't think about ourselves. All we thought about were the dogs.

We had to get the dogs.

Under the shack, we hold the dogs hostage until one or two of us crawl in to pull them out. New Orleans has crawlspaces under the homes because they can't build foundations. When you build a city below sea level, the only way to go is up.

Chuck and I stand right over Rachel. She's underneath our feet as we rip up more floorboards to make an opening big enough for her and the dogs. We're in the backroom of the house, and the place smells bad, like rotten food swollen with heat and decay. The walls are mottled black and gray with mold, and the furniture is bloated and broken. A large bed is upside down against the far wall, and a dresser blocks the opening to the next room, its drawers fractured and splintered, blackened clothing filling its insides. A large strip of wallpaper hangs loosely over one window. It is yellowed and torn. The highwater mark frames the room, a black/gray, speckled petri dish-looking border we saw everywhere we went. A single shaft of sunlight shines through a shriveled and shredded shade. I am in someone's house. I don't know if they lived or died. I don't think about it for long. What I did know is they were unlikely to return. The place was destroyed.

We're somewhere near the corner of Pouger and North Claiborne, but the exact address is unknown because we came in through the back. We entered from a side street and crawled through the thick overgrown brush—the same path the dogs took.

Rachel is talking sweet now. "Come here, boy. I won't hurt you."

Mud flies from the crawlspace as Rachel's legs kick faster. The dogs are cowering, three scared souls backed into the far corner, as far from her reach as they can possibly be. She's crawling through broken glass and trash; plumbing and floor joists create a maze that she must wiggle through. Rachel screams that she has found them, and my heart starts beating fast. I'm scared for Rachel, and I'm afraid for the dogs. Scared their first meeting won't go well.

At night, the dogs of New Orleans pack in open spaces. Schoolyards and parks were favorite places and provided safety from curious eyes or cruel people. Under the setting sun, we'd watch them from afar, taking notes of their numbers, sizes, and coloring. The next day, we'd discuss our plan to trap them in adjoining neighborhoods. Volunteers would fan out and cover all but one of the openings to the park. The rest of us would approach from three sides, hoping they would run in the direction we had not covered. We knew they'd find the first garage or house to crawl under, and we had already staked out the options. Despite our careful planning, they sometimes got away. They ran the streets like criminals who knew the neighborhood. Like they'd been running these streets for years. They knew every alley, driveway, and vacant garage. They knew the underbellies of houses.

The tougher ones growled and clawed the ground with their feet, like bulls preparing to rush the matador. They looked vicious, nervous, and scared. We were dirty, tired, and scared too. In the early days after the storm, we had very few tools. We'd crawl in from as many angles as possible, trapping them where they hid. If one of us had a catchpole, we were lucky. If not, we grabbed for any part of them while our words tried to convince them we meant no harm. One by one, we'd pull them out, our work synchronized as if we'd been doing this for years. Waiting hands in the sunlight held on tight until we safely got them into a crate. A little water and some food, and they were no longer the menacing beasts in the dark. They didn't bare their teeth or growl. They'd lie down when we told them to and lap at the water we put in a bowl at their feet. They ate every bit of food and let us touch their heads. They recognized help and hope.

Rachel's yelling, she's got one. I smile for the first time that day, knowing that the dog she has at the end of her catchpole has a chance now. Chuck and I jump down out of the shack to be there when she pulls him out. There's barely any room for her to retreat, so we furiously claw away more mud. The guy from the Associated Press moves quickly into position, filming every detail of the rescue. The end of her catchpole appears, and Troy grabs it. The only way for Rachel to get out is to get the dog out first. Troy wrestles with the pole as the dog on its end violently thrashes in a last-ditch effort to free himself. The dog writhes, and the mud flies. The cinch noose is tight around his neck. He struggles and flails, but Troy holds tight as the game of tug of war continues. The dog wants to attack, but the length of the pole prevents him from getting too close to us. We know we have to calm him down as quickly as possible because if we don't, he could break his neck on the noose.

The first dog we pulled that day is surprisingly small given the fight he put up, and his body is covered in mud. The whites of his eyes flicker against the brown and matted backdrop of his face. He's an unneutered male with short stumpy legs. He's shaking badly while we wipe the thick mud from around his eyes. His legs quiver, his steps tentative as we lead him to the road and gently load him into the back of the SUV. We give him cool water and a warm hand. Within minutes he calms and drinks from the bowl. He's one of three that packed, roamed, and scoured these post-Katrina streets that day. We tracked this pack for two hours that morning before trapping them under the shotgun shack. One down. Two to go.

It took us two more hours to save the three dogs. When Rachel finally emerged, she was covered head to toe in mud, her long brown hair muddy rivulets surrounding a beaming face. We congratulated one another, knowing we had saved them from a lonely and certain death. We laughed at the fear we all felt while she crawled into the unknown. We hugged each other, our smiles were broad, our exhilaration at our shared sense of accomplishment like a drug. The three dogs were lying in separate crates in the back of an air-conditioned SUV. They knew immediately we weren't going to do them any harm. They rested on the short drive back to Magazine, where they were bathed and fed. Later that day, they let us hold them and take them on short walks around the neighborhood. We put comforters in their crates, and they slept soundly.

As we were leaving the neighborhood, we saw a tattered, thin dog walk into a yard a few houses away. We followed. The house was unlivable with its walls blasted right open, revealing the broken insides. A clawfoot bathtub was in full view from the road. The dog had walked into the heavily vegetated backyard that showed signs of a dog being kept outside: a scum-filled stainless steel bowl and a rusty old chain attached to a fence. An "outside" dog, as I would later come to learn. A practice for many in the Deep South. She appeared to be old, and one of her eyes was severely infected. It wept as we slowly circled her. Her stomach and teats were distended, an indication she had mothered many litters. She looked like no one had loved her a day in her life. Like she'd lost all hope. She sat stoically still as the catchpole snare was placed gently around her neck. She offered no resistance as we slowly urged her to walk with us. Her head held high, she'd mustered whatever dignity remained. She looked profoundly sad and surrendered to her fate. This one really broke my heart. We walked her to one of the vehicles and picked her up and placed her inside. We drove her straight to one of the veterinary clinics. Her condition was poor, and her eye needed immediate attention. After we dropped her off, Laura and I were driving back to Hound Zero when she looked at me with tears in her eyes. "I am going to adopt her, Chris," she said. "She'll get the best care, and home I promise you that." That day we trapped nine dogs. And that night, we slept well, knowing that nine fewer dogs were trying to survive the streets of New Orleans.

Central City, just north of the Garden District, had been in decline for decades. A poor, working-class, mostly Black neighborhood, it was crime-ridden with blighted and abandoned buildings before the storm. And while it was on relatively high ground, and saw little flooding, it was virtually uninhabited after Katrina.

The next morning, we were asked if we could search for another pack of dogs living under a house in that neighborhood. We got the address and headed out. When we arrived, we donned our masks and gloves and asked who wanted to crawl under the house. Rachel and Cadi would be the team. The rest of us circled the house with our catchpoles and netting. Utility workers were working across the road and stopped what they were doing as we got to work. Rachel and Cadi began crawling under the house when suddenly the front door opened. I don't know who was more surprised—me at seeing someone living there or the young, Black woman looking at me with my shirt reading "Animal Rescue," baseball cap, and headlamp. I looked at her with a contrite smile.

"I am so sorry," I said. "We didn't realize people were living here."

"My grandma and I live here," she said. "We heard all kinds of commotion."

"Some dogs are living under your house," I said. "Would it be OK if we tried to catch them?"

"Oh, yes, we know about that," she replied.

And for the next hour and a half, we became the main attraction in the neighborhood. The young woman came outside and marveled at our amateur operation. At one point, her grandmother went to the door, a broad and beautiful smile on her face. She thanked us for helping the dogs she knew had been living under the house but didn't know what to do about it. "I can hear them at night," she told me.

The utility workers were all large, muscular men. The size of football players, their bright yellow vests and hardhats imposing, they looked so tough. And they couldn't believe it when Rachel and Cadi crawled under the house. They remarked on their courage. A few admitted they'd be reluctant to do the same. One said, "Oh, hell no, I wouldn't!" And when we pulled the dogs out, they took off their hardhats as if in salute and clapped. There's a picture taken of all of the Dogbusters that day and the young woman whose house it was. We're all arm in arm. We're dirty, exhausted, and smiling.

Chapter Seven

The Waveland Twenty-Six

Michelle Prince was born and raised in Colorado but lived just outside Biloxi, Mississippi, on August 29, 2005. Her then-husband, an air force nurse, was stationed at the nearby base and was in Germany at the time of Katrina. She evacuated with her kids, cats, and her dog, Mesa. A five-foot-nothing mother of two, she worked at the Humane Society of South Mississippi in Gulfport. The HSSM was located in an old army bunker out by the airport and adjacent to the sewage treatment plant READ: the least attractive acreage within city limits. Construction on their brand-new shelter was almost 100 percent complete when Katrina hit. Its proximity to the coast made it vulnerable to the flooding, but fortunately, the most significant damage it suffered was the wind. Even in their storm-battered bunker and recently acquired FEMA trailer, they were better-staffed and -funded than Waveland. Furthermore, their staff was compassionate and caring. At HSSM, it was never us versus them. The animals were our main concern. We all worked together.

Michelle and I hit it off immediately. Our shared passion for the animals gave us a solid foundation for a friendship that endured. She had been arranging transports for their animals while I was doing the same for mine. Many animal shelters across the United States wanted to help the animal victims of the hurricane, and we learned together how to get them there. From New York to Arizona, Denver to Oregon, there was available space in shelters across the country and communities of people who wanted to adopt a hurricane survivor.

One morning I was working at Hound Zero when Michelle called, asking if there were any available volunteers to help them set up a temporary shelter in a large field adjacent to the bunker. The Humane Society's kennels were always full, and animal control trappers from around the US had been asked if they could dispatch to Gulfport to assist in trapping animals that were still trying to survive on the streets. That day we had extra hands at Hound Zero, so a bunch of folks volunteered to go to Gulfport with me.

Later that night, after an exhausting day of setting up crates and tents, we stopped at a newly reopened Applebee's on I-49 in Gulfport. We were bone-tired and hungry for hot food. Minutes into my meal, my cell phone rang. It was a member of the In Defense of Animals Mississippi team. Chase had called, and Waveland had filled to capacity that day with more strays and unwanted litters of puppies. Roberta was threatening to "put them all down in the morning." I was asked if we could go and pull from Waveland. I had boots on the ground but no access to kennels and crates, and we had to act quickly. Fortunately, we would drive right by Waveland on our way back to New Orleans.

I went back to the table and explained what was happening. I asked if anyone wanted to go with me to Waveland. Everyone said yes. All they wanted to know was how they could help. I called Holly and asked if there was any way someone could meet us in Waveland with crates. She asked how many I wanted, and

I told her as many as possible. She told me she'd find someone and they'd meet us at the Waveland shelter. Within the hour, we were at Waveland: Sarah Rose, Cameron, Xiante, Carol, and Lis were with me, and shortly after arriving, Colleen Kessler and Jan Mitchell arrived from New Orleans with the Budget animal rescue van. It was loaded with crates. I had called Chase and asked if he'd meet us there to let us in and he met us at the front gate.

The first to go was a weeks-old puppy laying all alone on a dirty towel in a large, cold, concrete cage. There wasn't a chance in hell that baby would have made it through the night. I asked someone to grab a blanket and quickly wrapped the puppy in it. I called for Sarah Rose and handed her the pup telling her to go to the vehicle and hold the puppy close to her chest. That was her job; it was all she had to do. She took the pup-filled blanket and ran outside.

A few cages down a little border collie mix was alone in a kennel. She was standing with her back legs crossed. She looked like a tripod. I asked what was wrong with her legs, and Chase joked that was how she stood, that she was fine. He laughed. I didn't. It wasn't until we got her back to Hound Zero that we learned she had a dislocated hip and broken femur. She was the second to be taken outside to the van.

A one-eyed white hound mix, cowering in a corner, was surely going to be one of Roberta's first targets in the morning. No one was adopting in Hancock County, much less a scared-shitless one-eyed dog. Colleen crawled into his kennel as he lay down on the floor, terrified of her. We had to make a gurney out of a blanket to carry him to the van. He was too afraid to walk.

There were a coonhound mama dog and her large litter of puppies. They had no food or water, and we knew we'd take them too. I yelled to Chase that the large family was leaving. A few of my team sprang into action and started removing them from their concrete hell. A Rottweiler with severely infected eyes had to be left behind, why I don't know, but Chase said Roberta gave strict instructions he wasn't to leave with us that night. Xiante loves Rottweilers, and she asked if there was anything I could do. I was reluctant to push the matter. I asked Chase again and was told no. The poor dog's eyes were crusted with pus from an infection. His kennel floor was covered in urine and feces. We cleaned his eyes and cleaned up the mess. At that point, it was all we could do.

Lis, a vet tech from Washington State, started vaccinating the coonhound puppies. They'd have to have some protection, as would the others at Hound Zero, and now that they were technically ours, we wanted them to have the best possible start. As a rule, the shelter didn't vaccinate.

Chase was in the back room with Lis helping her with the pups, and Carol Guzy was shooting photos while Xiante, Colleen, Jan, and I continued to walk through the kennels. There was a little black female that I had attempted to pull several times before, and each time I asked, Roberta said no. She knew how much I wanted to help that dog and, whether to discourage me or show who was boss, that little dog had been in there for at least a month.

The first time I saw her, her water bowl was half-empty, and the water inside was dirty, a light green film floating on top. She had no food. She was so little and scared, and when I reached to her, she let me touch her. Her body looked strong, but the white around her nose told me she had been through hard times. She didn't look old. She looked young, helpless, and alone. I whispered to her through the diamond-shaped wires of the door to her cage. I promised I would get her out of there.

That night I did. I didn't ask Chase if I could take her, I told him. He knew I'd grown attached to her, and he didn't object.

Xiante and I walked to her kennel, and I opened the rusted chain-link door for the last time. I placed a gentle lead around her neck and kneeled on the floor to look into her eyes. Xiante touched my arm as my tears fell. After a minute or two, Xiante walked her out to one of our vans.

That night a few weary but elated souls saved twenty-six animals from certain death. The space we created ensured the threat of euthanizing animals had been reduced. In our group were the one-eyed dog and the little border collie mix who was checked as soon as we got back to Hound Zero. We made as comfortable a bed for her as we could, knowing we couldn't take her to a vet hospital until the next day.

We took sixteen puppies. Sarah's puppy was so young it had to be bottle-fed. We took some kittens and a few adult cats.

It was after midnight by the time we got everyone packed and loaded for the ride back to New Orleans. I called Holly and told her we were coming, and we would need help unloading the animals. It didn't matter what time we arrived, she said, they'd be waiting. We got back at 3:00 a.m., and Hound Zero came alive again.

One block north of Hound Zero, 1202 Felicity Street had been vacant since the storm. A three-family house with a large one-bedroom apartment on the main floor, it had been offered to us. Sleeping bags, air mattresses, and a few cots were placed close together so as many as possible could rest in a real "home" safe from the elements and with a toilet and running water. We even had electricity. Most nights, we also had a menagerie of cats and dogs living with us.

Carol and I had decided to name my little black dog Hope. Exhausted after the emergency situation at Waveland, we took her to the apartment with us. Most of us slept in sleeping bags on the floor. There were a few cots, from where I don't know, and hot water for showers. We took turns showering before trying to get some sleep. Most of us did so quickly, but when Xiante took her turn, I could hear her crying in the shower. Xiante cried for a very long time.

That night I lay on an air mattress on the floor with Hope wrapped in a blanket by my side. She'd been through enough in her young life, and I wanted her to feel as comfortable and safe as possible. As I worked on my laptop, she slept soundly.

I couldn't sleep. The screen of my laptop projected enough light for me to continue working until the sun began to rise. There were emails to answer and transports to schedule. The opportunities to remove animals from the area needed to be filled because chances were they'd dry up soon enough. Hope was fast asleep. Occasionally I would reach over and pet her soft fur. I had been pulling dogs and cats out of Waveland for two months at that point, and I still couldn't grasp the apathy I had witnessed. It made no sense that I would be denied saving the little black dog beside me or having to leave the Rottweiler behind. I gave him the name Phoenix. He deserved a name. I knew full well I'd never see that poor baby again.

I wanted to have sympathy for the people I most loathed in Waveland. They had returned home and most had lost everything. Roberta lived in a FEMA trailer in her backyard. Tori and Larry still had their apartments, but they couldn't possibly be immune to the tragedy surrounding them. Although they never spoke of it, their city was gone. The schools were closed, the stores were boarded up, churches vanished, and entire blocks had washed away. Neighbors, co-workers, and childhood friends fled, never to return. The death toll in southern Mississippi was approximately 238 people. But try as I might, I still could not get past the cruelty and apathy. The horror predated the current staff and was something few in the community felt they could change. I met some of those folks in my travels, and the stories I was told cannot be repeated here. They are incomprehensible: Days-old puppies left alone in cold, hard cages, without the ability to eat or drink on their own. Hosing down the kennels with the animals in them, watery feces and urine splattering their bodies. The blaring country music and nonexistent human touch or comfort. When the staff evacuated the shelter before the storm, they shut the doors behind them. No attempt was made to save them. The animals drowned.

I didn't want to understand how someone could see so much suffering and do nothing. I didn't want it to be forgivable; I wanted it to be impossible. I'd spent hours in the company of individuals who got paid to run the shelter. The safety of the animals fell on them. Roberta, Tori, Larry, and Chase were the only ones in a position to save the abandoned and neglected, and they did little to nothing. When I was there, the animals were held and cared for. The blaring music was lowered or put on a station playing classical or even NPR. They had clean water and fresh food. But as soon as I left, all bets were off. It was almost too much to bear.

After a few hours' sleep, I was once again standing in front of Holly's makeshift podium as she prepared us for the day. I checked on the Waveland 25 (Hope was still at the apartment), and everyone was doing well. We named the one-eyed dog One-Eyed Jack, and a young couple from New York City had cared for him during the night. They wanted to bring him home with them. He still wouldn't walk. The border collie had indeed been suffering, and his dislocated hip required an emergency hospital outside of the city. The puppies and their mama were happy in a large crate with clean water, and plenty of food, and the cats and kittens were purring at every touch. It was an excellent start to another day.

By December 2005, I was spending most of my time in Mississippi. Michelle and I had become good friends, and I had been invited to stay at her house whenever I was down south. Every day it was the same routine: work at the shelter, move animals from Waveland to Gulfport, pick up takeout, and head home to have dinner with her two kids.

A steady stream of Waveland babies had been able to leave on transport, primarily when rescuers were leaving town to return to their prospective cities. No one left the coast empty-handed. And with the help of two young men from Waveland, William and Dorty, we had been able to run a few transports to upstate New York, which thrilled William to no end since his life-long dream was to see Niagara Falls. William and Dorty drove our animals all over the country, and not once did we pay them. We couldn't afford to. The donations I received had to be used for veterinary bills, gas, rental vans, and vaccines.

I worked to exhaustion. We all did. The steady stream of animals never stopped, and while the surrenders and strays were bad in Waveland, it was even worse in Gulfport. More people were living in Gulfport, and it was a much larger city. Every day we faced more and more surrendered animals.

One day a pickup truck backed up to the surrender area. There was a dog in a crate in the bed. A man jumped out of the cab. I remember his muscular, sunburned arms and dirty jeans, but not his name. When asked why he was surrendering his pet, he complained that Maggie wouldn't stop urinating in the house, "even after hitting her with a newspaper." I disliked him immediately. I walked Maggie to the outside kennels because the ones inside were full. I opened the door to the cage and promised the confused little dog it would only be until the morning: I had a scheduled transport the next day, and come hell or high water, Maggie would be on it. It hurt me to think that this sweet dog was being dumped at the shelter to be caged, cold and confused, through the chilly December night after having lived in the warmth of her own home.

I walked back inside and found Maggie's owner filling out paperwork. He turned to me and asked if he could see Maggie one last time. On the walk out back, he told me that since Katrina, things had been hard. He had lost his job and now his home. The family was going to move in with relatives in Denver. He didn't want to put Maggie through more upheaval, and what if they ended up someplace where they couldn't keep her? When he saw her in the cage, he started to cry. I placed my hand on his shoulder and told him she would only be there one night. "We have transport to Massachusetts tomorrow," I told him. "I promise she'll be on it." He asked if I would please call him when she made it to Massachusetts and found her new home. I watched him walk away with his head hung low, no longer the bully I had presumed him to be. He was just one more casualty of the storm, having to make impossible choices to survive. I called him a few weeks later and emailed him a picture of Maggie playing in the New England snow.

I wanted to be home for Christmas, so I decided to drive to take animals with me. Robyn Ochs and Peg Preble, two dear friends from Massachusetts, lived in a close-knit community in the Jamaica Plain neighborhood of Boston, and they had reached out to their neighbors asking if any wanted to adopt a new pet. Althea flew to Gulfport so I wouldn't have to drive alone. Within just a few days, and with the help of Robyn and Peg, we had enough good homes to place thirty-three animals: cats, dogs, kittens, and puppies. Maggie had a new home too. I met Althea at the airport, and we headed over to Enterprise on I-49. All they had available was a passenger van with four rows of bench seats. It was going to be tight, but it would have to do.

It was a cold December morning when we left Gulfport, our passenger van crammed tight with animal crates in every available space. It was the same morning I said goodbye to my Hope. One of the rescuers in Gulfport had an aunt in Virginia who wanted to adopt her, and she was headed up that way to go home herself. She'd take Hope with her. Once again, I hit my knees and looked into her eyes. My tears fell as I told her I'd miss her and that everything was going to be OK now. I said it for me as much as I did for her.

It took us thirty-six hours to make it home. We stopped frequently to walk the dogs and scoop the litterboxes and make sure everyone was OK. Althea would drive, and I'd try to sleep, but I was too exhausted, and the adrenaline coursing through my veins made rest impossible. Sleeping in the van was uncomfortable as well. In the early morning hours, fatigue took its toll with my eyesight and stamina, but I couldn't rest. Our first stop was in Maryland, where we met the adopters for one of the

HSSM puppies, the adoption prearranged by the folks at the shelter. Next up was a rest area on I-90 in Massachusetts, where we dropped off two HSSM puppies, both to Massachusetts homes that I'd found through the emails I'd been sending out since mid-September. After a few quick pictures of the puppies with their new families, we headed east to Boston.

It was brutally cold that December night when we finally pulled up to the home of one of Robyn and Peg's neighbors. The curtain in the front picture window pulled back and expectant, smiling faces peered out. The front door opened, and streams of people poured out of the home and excitedly circled our van. Twenty-five of the animals were cats and kittens, but the five dogs that had homes waiting for them were taken off the van first. The joy of their new families was palpable. The cats and kittens were brought inside where everyone picked out their new family members as Althea, and I looked on, weary but relieved. As much as we wanted to stay and watch the adoption process unfold, we were so exhausted it was all we could do to walk over to Robyn and Peg's and fall into bed. It was the best sleep I'd had in more than two months.

Chapter Eight

Priorities

Christmas in New England is typically a cold, white affair. By the winter of 2005, I had moved and was living in my uncle's house in North Eastham on Cape Cod. Honey Bear Belle was recovering from her heartworm treatment, and my Team Sheltie—Macy, Demi, and I—were enjoying the peace and quiet of a Cape Cod offseason. The days were cold, but the snow had yet to arrive.

The last three months working on the Gulf Coast had been exhilarating and devastating. Every day I worried about the animals and the folks who were still arriving or had never left—the catastrophe that was Katrina. In daily contact with Michelle in Gulfport and friends in New Orleans, we were still organizing transports throughout the United States.

Early Christmas morning, I left the Cape and headed to my brother's home northwest of Boston, for the day. While driving through downtown Boston, my phone rang. It was Tara High, the director of HSSM. I had gotten close to Tara and her sisters during the days working at her shelter. Before I left to come home Tara had invited me to their family Christmas celebration. Her sister's home north of the interstate had suffered only minimal damage and it was brightly decorated with Christmas lights inside and out. It was wonderful to be part of a family Christmas in the southern tradition and to experience something as heartwarming as a family gathering. It was a stark contrast to the world I had been mired in for weeks.

She told me she knew of a dog who was gravely injured at the Waveland Animal Shelter. She said she had been unable to sleep the night before knowing she had to do something. She asked if I could help getting him out of there.

I called Chase and woke him. I asked him what was going on with the injured dog in the shelter. He told me the dog had been brought in by animal control after getting hit by a car. A Good Samaritan had tried to help the dog, but when they tried to move him, no doubt in pain, he bit. Because of the bite incident, Roberta was not only denying medical care but refusing to humanely euthanize the dog. She said she was legally obligated to hold the dog on a "rabies-hold" and there was no funding to bring him to a vet. I asked Chase to sit tight while I called Tara back. We came up with a plan. Tara called her shelter veterinarian and asked if she could go to the shelter for an emergency. I called Chase and asked if he would please bring the injured dog to HSSM. He dressed and drove to the Waveland shelter. At this point, none of us cared what Roberta would do. We did what had to be done.

I arrived at my brother's home, and the dog had been taken to HSSM, where the vet immediately determined he was suffering from a severe head injury. And while Chase waited, she made the compassionate decision to euthanize him. And while that brought me some sense of relief, it also saddened me deeply. And, as my young nephews and niece celebrated the day by opening their presents and as my family and I looked on, I couldn't help but feel detached from it all. By then, the horror and disbelief had shaken my naïve belief in the goodness of people. Every waking moment all I could think about was a far and distant place, so unlike anything I had ever known.

In the coming months, neither Roberta nor I mentioned the Christmas rescue. I don't know what happened when she returned to work and I didn't really want to know. Confronting her about the injured dog would have pissed her off and a power struggle would have ensued. Chase and I didn't speak about it except for when I thanked him for all he had done that day. Tara and I cried on the phone together on my ride back to Cape Cod but we never spoke of it again.

I had applied for nonprofit charity status with the federal government for the newly formed Animal Rescue Front. The name was born from the many emails I sent to inform friends of the frontlines of Katrina. When my sister was in New Orleans, she often worked side by side with the military. There were pictures of military vehicles driven up to the windows of homes so the rescuers could climb up and crawl in them. Sometimes they helped my sister break down doors. One day the soldiers, rifles slung over their shoulders, were crawling under a porch saying, "Come here, kitty, kitty." She laughed when she told that story. Encounters with the military were frequent and friendly. Most of them loved animals too.

From my home on Cape Cod, I was still coordinating transports out of the Gulf, and the connections I had made throughout the United States kept me very busy. But a professional job opening had presented itself in my town, and I applied.

I got the job.

I hadn't had permanent full-time work as an information technology professional since 2001, when I walked away from a six-figure salary and a hostile environment to women as the vice president of communications for a major financial corporation. It was two-weeks prior to 9/11, and there was no way of knowing that tragedy and the subsequent reverberations would keep me out of viable employment for the next five years. I was excited and relieved to secure full-time work. The salary was decent and the industry was in healthcare. I had benefits again.

I lasted for five weeks.

Overqualified, it was a steady paycheck and on Cape Cod, a difficult environment to find professional employment, and I had gotten lucky. But, hard as I tried, I was unable to focus on anything but the crushing need of the animals. I was obsessed with imagining what was happening in Mississippi and New Orleans. I thought of the people, hundreds of thousands of Americans were displaced or worse, and the animals were still dying on the streets of New Orleans and Mississippi. One day the head of human resources barreled into my office, her face red, her mouth nearly frothing. She threw some sheets of paper on my desk. They were records from a vet's office where two gravely injured Waveland animals had been taken. I was trying to get funding from one of the larger organizations that had received millions of dollars in animal rescue donations, and I needed the invoices. I saw no harm in a few sheets of paper. But she made it very clear that the company fax machine and paper were never to be used for personal business. While I respected this, it felt like an extreme overreaction. I thought she was going to fire me on the spot.

Try as I might, my professional responsibilities felt secondary in importance, and a few weeks later, I realized I refused to live in a world in which a broken printer spelled disaster. It came to a head the day I was called to deal with a printer issue in the clinic's admitting office. The desktop printer had malfunctioned, and all hell broke loose. There was a second printer in that office, but it was located six feet away. The staff was incredulous when I told them it would have to serve as the printing option until we could get the vendor in to fix the broken unit. I looked into their horrified faces, and at that moment, I knew I was done. I couldn't stay there one day longer. Animals were suffering and neglected in a hurricane-ravaged and condemned shelter. I went back to my office, packed my things, verbally resigned, and left.

The situation that ultimately led to my professional demise started in late January. Late one night, my phone shook me awake. It took a minute for me to surface through the fog of sleep and recognize the gravelly voice of one of the Mississippi volunteers for In Defense of Animals. "I just got a call from Chase," she said. "There are some animals in horrible shape in Waveland." Chase's motives were sometimes suspect. I sensed he played both sides and rumors he was a dogfighter were impossible to reconcile. But in cases like this, I found his sly allegiances useful. After all, he had gone in on Christmas Day and helped that poor dog. Chase had given me his cell phone number. It was too late to call him, and I knew it would have to wait until morning. Morning couldn't come soon enough.

The next morning, I called Roberta. I swallowed my anger and had a personal commitment to keeping my daily calls friendly and nonchalant, "just checking in" to see how we might help ease poor Roberta's burden. My acting skills were becoming quite impressive. So was my ability to gauge the safety of the animals based on the state of Roberta's mood. Puppies set her off the most. The motherless litters that arrived at Waveland in buckets or laundry baskets were often sickly and too tiny to be on their own. They whimpered and tumbled around in their own waste. They demanded more care than Roberta or her staff was willing to begrudge. Since FEMA had installed a trailer for the staff to use as an office, Roberta, Tori, and Larry felt even less need than usual to waste any of their time inside the actual shelter, tending to animals which, Roberta complained loudly, "are just going to shit all over the place again anyway."

My objective had always been to sweep in and clear the cages by getting the animals to Hound Zero or Gulfport. Pragmatism wasn't the only thing choreographing the steps to this tortured tango with Roberta. Roberta's fall to the bottom of the municipal hierarchy left her prone to exerting control wherever she could. On this particular morning, however, her mood seemed no uglier than usual, and the number of animals she claimed to be sheltering was low enough not to set off any alarms. It sounded like we might have a little time to line up safe placements for everyone before making another emergency late-night shelter run.

I moved on to the real reason I had called. "How many medicals do you have?" I asked. Roberta knew we would give priority to any animal in need of veterinary care. We always pulled the medicals first.

"None," she answered.

"None?" I pressed.

"Yes," she confirmed. "No medicals."

We hung up. She was lying. Chase had no reason to make that up. Here was my payback for the Christmas rescue: a pointed reminder that Roberta was the one in charge. But I had a bigger point to make, and I was tired of playing nice. I called Michelle in Gulfport. I asked her if she could go to the shelter late that night and photograph the animals. Michelle's friendship, tireless efforts, and dedication had made her ARF's unofficial second-in-command. I trusted her implicitly.

"Can you go to Waveland tonight after hours and take some pictures?" I asked.

"Yes," she answered without hesitation.

"You have to be very careful," I warned. "If you get caught we're screwed. I have no idea if the police are patrolling back there or if Roberta has installed a camera. Disguise yourself. Wear a hat and tuck your hair up."

Michelle and I both knew it wasn't us who had the most to lose if she got caught—it was the animals. I called the IDA volunteer to give her an update. "I'm sending someone in tonight," I said. "Make sure we have access."

That evening, Chase left Waveland's newly installed chain-link gate unlocked, and Michelle went in and photographed two critically injured dogs. Walker, a gorgeous coonhound, had suffered a severe head injury. The left side of his scalp, including his ear, was hanging in a jagged, bloody mess. Buddy, an adorable yellow Lab mix not even six months old, was a few cages down from Walker. His cage was filled with urine-soaked towels and feces, and he couldn't sit or stand. His water can had a brown, sludge-like substance in the bottom, and the threadbare towel he lay on was soaked in urine. When Michelle approached his cage, his tail began to wag and he pulled his broken body to get closer to her. Michelle photographed both dogs and the conditions they were in. Then she knelt on the filthy concrete floor to offer what comfort she could to the little yellow Lab, gently stroking his dirty fur and talking to him gently through her own tears.

Neither dog had food, and their water cans were empty, but Michelle knew she couldn't leave fresh water or fill their bowls with food. The next morning the staff would notice. And even though the gate had been left unlocked, we were breaking the law. Michelle finally pulled herself away and left. "It was the hardest thing I've ever had to do," she told me later that night.

Within a few hours, the emails with pictures began arriving in my inbox. I sent the most-disturbing images to Doll Stanley, the animal cruelty investigator for the state of Mississippi. For good measure, I emailed them to television stations in Jackson and Gulfport as well. Then I prayed for Roberta to find herself in a major shitstorm first thing the next morning.

The next day Doll Stanley arrived at the Waveland Animal Shelter at 9:00 a.m., trailing a news crew from WLOX and a media investigative team from Jackson. Their cameras were rolling when they found Roberta and Tori hanging out in Roberta's new shiny office in the FEMA trailer. An outraged Roberta immediately shot up from her chair and thrust her hand in front of the cameras, ordering the crews to stop filming, a directive they calmly ignored. Roberta dialed the city attorney for reinforcement and was informed the media had a right to be there. Doll demanded to see the animals in the shelter. Fuming, Roberta had no choice but to comply.

Doll found what amounted to numerous violations of even minimal animal care. But in Mississippi, there was no code of care or conduct in the sheltering of animals. Doll questioned the lack of identifying documentation and the conditions of the cages and of the animals. When she found the two injured dogs, she confronted Roberta on camera.

"Why haven't these animals gotten any medical attention?" Doll wanted to know.

"I was going to call the vet today," Roberta countered.

After reprimanding the staff and reminding them of some basic requirements for animal shelters in Mississippi, Doll left with the cameras in tow. She called me minutes later.

"Can you get them out of there?" she asked.

"Yes," was my reply.

That night on the six o'clock news, WLOX ran footage of Buddy trying to crawl in his cage. Walker's wound was blurred out; it was too disturbing for TV. When Doll made her rounds that morning, she had also observed two cats that were in obvious distress as well. One appeared to have a fractured jaw and the other was very ill with an upper respiratory infection, her eyes and nose crusted with mucus. Fortunately, I didn't have to worry about any of them. Within an hour of Doll's departure, I had orchestrated their release from the Waveland Animal Shelter.

Getting the newly named Buddy and Walker and the two sick cats out was not going to be easy. Roberta quickly put two and two together, beginning with my persistent asking of the "do you have any medicals" the day before. She hadn't seen the pictures yet, and as soon as she did, she'd know we were in the shelter that night. As soon as Doll left, Roberta rounded up her staff and forbade them to talk with or cooperate in any way with rescuers. She was emphatic that no one was to have any contact whatsoever with me in particular. She threatened to check their city-issued cell phone records to enforce the ban. Chase called to give me his wife's cell phone number right after the edict was delivered and warned me not to call him again on his city-issued phone. Roberta had threatened to fire anyone who spoke with me.

I sorted through my contact list and called a staffer I knew at an animal clinic in New Orleans. A native New Orleanian and owner of two vacation properties that were destroyed during Katrina, she agreed to call and try to talk Roberta into surrendering the animals to them. Within an hour she called back. Roberta had accepted her offer to "take the animals causing all that trouble off your hands," but only on one condition: they could not come to me, or anyone affiliated with ARF. It was a promise easily made and more easily broken.

Lucy Pribbenow was a pistol of a redhead from Alaska who headed straight for the Gulf post-Katrina and never looked back. By January 2006, she had been in New Orleans for five months and had no intention of leaving. Lucy had a reputation as the one willing to do anything to help out. At five-feet tall, she was tough as an Alaskan winter. She made it her business to stay plugged-in and on-call. Once I knew the animals would be surrendered, I had to find someone to get them. I called Celebration Station. Luckily, Lucy was there and they handed her the phone. With explicit instructions not to mention anything other than to say she was driving them to the clinic in New Orleans, she set up one of the vehicles with water, and bedding. A few hours later, she called to confirm that the "Waveland Four" were safely in her van.

As soon as they arrived at the clinic in New Orleans, it was immediately determined they needed emergency care an ordinary vet's office could not provide. A specialty hospital on the Northshore of Lake Pontchartrain was called, and Lucy headed there.

Buddy's hip was dislocated, and his femur was shattered. The emergency doctor surmised he had been hit by a car. Buddy had been in excruciating pain for eight days by the time we found him, and his injuries would require extensive surgery. But given the conditions he had been in, he was too weak to survive such an operation. It was going to take a few days to manage his pain and get the swelling down to perform surgery. He needed to be hydrated and to put some weight on. Walker was going to need skin grafts to close the gaping wound on his head, but he would recover and heal "just fine," they said. One of the cats had a fractured jaw that required surgery, and the other had a severe upper respiratory infection they were confident would go away with a round of antibiotics.

I asked how much Buddy's surgery would cost.

Five thousand dollars was the conservative estimate. I gave my permission, knowing full well we didn't have that kind of money. We were barely getting by with the small donations that periodically came in, and my credit card limit had been maxed out since November. I was more than $12,000 in debt already, and I'd only been at this for three months.

In desperation, I called Pia Salk, one of the founders of Animal Rescue New Orleans, the new name of Jane Garrison's group on Magazine, and asked if she knew how we might get some funding. In less than an hour, she called back with unbelievable news: Best Friends would pay for all the medical costs, not only for Buddy but for Walker and the two cats, as well. I couldn't believe what I was hearing. Tears of relief and joy cascading down my face all I could say was "thank you, thank you."

The cats recuperated quickly and were put up for adoption. As soon as Walker could leave the hospital, he went home with Michelle. Buddy's surgery was touch and go and required intensive inpatient care at the emergency hospital, but he pulled through, his leg crudely put back together with a metal plate and twelve screws. Buddy would be hospitalized for four weeks, and our plan was to get him north as soon as possible. But he wouldn't be able to travel for at least two months. As soon as he was ready, he was going to move in with me on the Cape.

In the meantime, I decided to lay low for a while. The events of the last few days had created a firestorm for the Waveland shelter staff. They were now under an intensified scrutiny from Roberta and my disdain for her neglect of the animals and the pain they had suffered, left me feeling very angry. I didn't make my daily calls.

Chase frequently called from his wife's cell phone to give me updates. Roberta was threatening legal action against the animal rescuers. She didn't want us anywhere near the property. As far as she was concerned, all we had done was cause trouble for them.

During the fallout, another local reached out to me. She had briefly worked at the shelter, and her boyfriend was on the Waveland police force. She told me there was talk around the station about a warrant for my arrest. Roberta had seen the pictures of Buddy and Walker on the evening news, and she knew someone had taken the photos after hours. In her mind, I was the most likely suspect. My alibi was bulletproof: I was home on Cape Cod when the pictures were taken. But Roberta didn't know that. She was pissed off, and she wanted someone to pay for her trouble. Trespassing and breaking and entering were rumored to be the likely charges I could face. I wasn't sure what to do or how I could find out if there was a warrant for my arrest, so I did the next best thing. I booked a flight to New Orleans.

Saving the Waveland 26. Waveland, Mississippi. Hope.

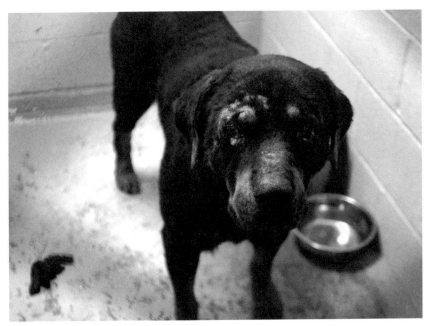

Phoenix, Waveland, Mississippi. They refused us permission to take him with us. Xiante cried a thousand tears that night in the shower. All we could do was listen.

Providing whatever vet care we could as we got the Waveland 26 to safety.

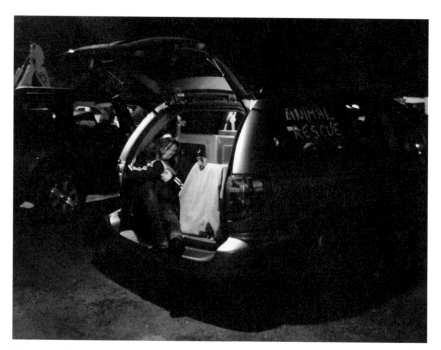

Xiante comforting one of the Waveland 26 puppies.

Sarah Rose with a newborn puppy that would have died had we not intervened.

Xiante and Chris McLaughlin the moment I know Hope was finally going to be ok.

Lis in Waveland, Mississippi, pulling a dog to safety.

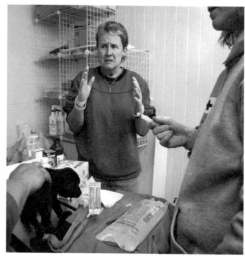

Colleen Kessler comforting One-Eyed Jack so he'd trust us to carry him out of the shelter.

The coonhound mama and her puppies were filled with parasites. Sometimes the reality was hard to bear.

The coonhound mama and her puppies.

A moment of sadness holding our dear Trixie.

The animals lived in and among us.

The sheet has patches from the many teams that traveled from all over the US to converge on an abandoned and forgotten city. Celebration Station, safe haven, home to heroes.

Every single creature mattered.

Getting ready to say goodbye to Trixie.

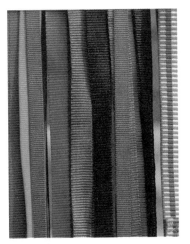

Color in the darkness.

Traci Dawson and Chris McLaughlin in a lighter moment as we get ready to leave for Gulfport, Mississippi.

Saying goodbye to Red, the paralyzed pit bull.

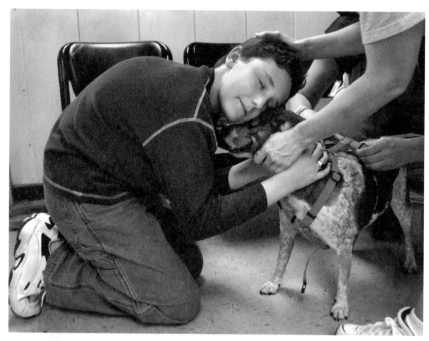

A boy and his doggie. Reunited.

Stray doggies struggling to survive in the devastation of Gulfport, Mississippi.

Manny, an animal control officer from Massachusetts, saving a dog from an abandoned home in Biloxi, Mississippi.

Loading up at the Humane Society of South Mississippi, the day Althea and Chris McLaughlin left with thirty-three babies headed to Massachusetts.

Safe at last.

Hope in my rented SUV. Gulfport, Mississippi.

Waveland, Mississippi—forgotten city of Katrina; the Mississippi Gulf Coast—forgotten story of Katrina.

A night of fun. One of the few. Late March 2006.

One of the lasting images I'll never forget. The high water mark in a destroyed home.

A little girl whose family dog was killed by sheriff's deputies in St. Bernard Parish.

Honoring the lives lost.

Trixie.

The moment I knew Honey Bear Belle belonged to Woody.

Chapter Nine

Celebration Station

Ten miles north of downtown, just off Interstate 10 in Metairie, Celebration Station was the new home for animal rescue in the greater New Orleans area. A giant disco and game arcade abandoned since the storm, it was a significant upgrade from Hound Zero. It had a cafeteria-style kitchen and dining area, and, with two floors, the upstairs was used for rest and sleep. With its leak-free roof, running water, and electricity, it offered us most of the comforts of home. A large parking lot surrounded the building, and an elaborate outside kennel area was built. As a result, we had more room to house the animals until they were evaluated and transported out of Louisiana.

Located on Veteran's Boulevard, just minutes from Louis Armstrong Airport, it was in a relatively unscathed section of greater New Orleans. Out on "Vet-er-an's," as the locals liked to say, there were coffee shops, stores, and a few restaurants, and our culinary selections increased substantially. After months in the Lower Garden District, where our options were limited to burritos and warm Power-C vitamin drink, many mornings someone would run to a satellite Cafe Du Monde and bring back bags of white-powered beignets and fresh chicory coffee. We were in heaven.

Metairie was an oasis of choices, and when I stumbled on the Borders bookstore, I was psyched. Books had been my escape since I was a little girl, and when I got overwhelmed or exhausted, I'd go to Borders and browse the aisles. Sometimes I'd just sit in a comfortable chair, close my eyes, and imagine that the horror just outside the door was very far away.

Security guards patrolled Celebration Station, and a security checkpoint refused entrance to anyone who couldn't give a valid reason to be there. Theft of our animals was a concern because pit bulls had been stolen out of the Lamar Dixon location in the earliest days after the hurricane. Compared to Hound Zero, this was luxury at its finest.

Celebration Station offered us all we'd need to sleep, shower, and shelter ourselves and the animals. The parking lot allowed for rows and rows of kennels where our animals had protection from the streets and the sun. Inside, in one of the larger rooms, there was a cat area where the felines could be kept safe and quiet. A restricted area was set up for medical treatment, and we used it to triage or quarantine sick animals. Celebration Station became the space for one large happy family, united in a common goal that the animals on the streets of New Orleans would suffer no more. And during my fourth trip to the coast, while I tried to find out if there was a warrant for my arrest in Mississippi, it became my home.

I arrived in late February 2006, and Carol Guzy was the first to welcome me back. After a quick hug, she grabbed my hand.

"I have to show you something, come on," she urged, barely pausing to let me drop my gear.

I followed her as she wove her way through the main lobby, where people were busy walking dogs, carrying supplies, and sitting and chatting around a long buffet table. We entered a caged area that looked like an exam room at a veterinarian's office, through a restroom area, and finally to a smaller room where shiny stainless-steel kennels lined one wall. Carol stopped at the last one, her thin, tired face breaking into a wide grin. Inside, a small puppy lay on a puffy little bed, surrounded by toys. "This is Trixie," Carol beamed. She opened the cage door and reached inside, gently pulling out Trixie and holding the little puppy to her chest. The first thing I noticed was Trixie's soulful brown eyes. She had a pug's face without the flattened nose. Carol had grabbed a soft blanket on our way to Trixie's kennel, and she wrapped her in it. It was then I noticed Trixie's front legs. They were bent at inward angles as if both had been broken. Her front paws curled against each other, forming a heart shape.

"What happened to her?" I gasped.

Carol explained that Trixie had been born with her front legs severely deformed. She was found at the Jefferson Parish Animal Shelter, where an animal rescue volunteer intervened. Trixie most certainly would have been euthanized. She was brought to Celebration Station and Best Friends, and Animal Rescue New Orleans had teamed up to take responsibility for her care. Trixie had quickly become everyone's favorite. Vets had been consulted, but it would require expensive testing to determine why her legs were twisted. That was a luxury we didn't have in a post-apocalyptic New Orleans, so the brain trust of local volunteers—with the expert advice of the veterinarians and vet techs among us—had to get creative.

Carol led me outside. A large plastic tub had been purchased, and every day, Trixie had water therapy. Someone would hold her while the puppy instinctively treaded water in her makeshift hydrotherapy pool. I had arrived just in time for her next water therapy session. "Team Trixie" gathered around to cheer her on while one of the guys held her in the water. Carol snapped away with her camera and, predictably, had fallen madly in love with her subject. I could see why. Watching that sweet, scrappy little puppy obediently paddle away was as emotional an experience as I had had since arriving in New Orleans. Before the storm, a puppy like Trixie would never have survived; she would have been dumped like trash.

Some of us wondered if her deformity was a result of the environmental havoc the flooding had caused in New Orleans. I remembered how the expensive new Merrell hiking boots I had purchased for my second trip had to be thrown away after only a few weeks of trudging through the muck. Who knew what poisons we were exposing ourselves to daily, wriggling around under condemned houses, chasing feral dog packs through the ankle-deep soup of who knew how much hazardous waste.

Trixie, imperfect but resilient, was something this city, held hostage by despair, had needed more than anything: proof of life. It didn't take long for Carol and me to start bending the Celebration Station rules to sneak Trixie up to our living area in the second-floor mezzanine. The mezzanine resembled a camp-ground—people had erected tents, laid down sleeping bags, or threw a few air mattresses together. Every night Carol and I would wait for the day's activities to quiet down before one of us would sneak downstairs to Trixie's kennel. She was small and easy to hide as we'd tuck her under a loose sweatshirt or jacket. Carol had staked out a spot in the mezzanine that looked down on the large entryway and common area below. We tied a sheet off over the railing to keep her camera equipment out of view and provide some privacy. I grabbed an abandoned air mattress and made a bed. We took turns sleeping with Trixie.

Damn, that place became home. I'd guess there were sixty of us living there on any given day. Folks bringing in abandoned animals and returning residents sometimes finding their own. Playtime with the doggies, and the cats frolicking in a completely caged in jungle-gym area while practicing all their feline antics. I'd fall asleep at night listening to the animals settle in, knowing I was doing something to ease the hurt in this forsaken city. Exhaustion was a constant, like a bone-dead, head-fog, what-is-my-name fatigue, but none of that mattered for any of us.

On one of those nights, I lay on my mattress and became overcome with a sense of well-being. Something like peace and hope all mixed up with the idea that everything was right with the world. I'd never felt that before. I heard the hushed voices of my friends and the occasional small bark from a dog. People were packing up or arriving. Another day lay ahead, and no one knew what it would bring. On that night, though, my experience of Katrina cemented my resolve that I would do everything I could for as long as I had to make this world a better place for animals. I'd go back to Waveland even if there was a warrant for my arrest. I'd shout, fight, and piss people off if I had to. People along the way might hate me, but I didn't care. For once, I just didn't give a shit anymore what anyone thought about me.

Best Friends had sent their IT person to New Orleans, and he set up a local area network. In a staged area off the main foyer were tables, and a few desks, and Juliette and Jason Watt, the Best

Friends coordinators, had a decent-sized operations area. The kitchen served food all day, and at night we'd try to sit down and have dinner together. If someone wasn't hungry, we'd ask them why. Everyone watched out for each other. We paid attention to silences and tears. In the office area, there were aquariums where a few exotic pets like reptiles and aquarium fish lived. They had been rescued too. We didn't leave anything behind.

By February, more people were returning to New Orleans, and many of them were still hoping to locate their pets. One morning Carol asked me to take her to the airport for a reunion between a young boy and his dog. The boy and his family were from St. Bernard Parish—their home had flooded, the family had to be rescued from their roof by the Coast Guard. They thought their dog drowned. But the Stealth Volunteers had found their small beagle mix in a foster home in Denver, and he was on a flight to New Orleans that day.

The boy and his parents were anxiously excited as we awaited the arrival. Soon a crate was pulled into the cargo area, and the father opened the gate. But when the dog was let out, he stood there frozen and confused. The boy kept calling his name, urging him to jump into his arms, only to dissolve into tears when he realized that his dog no longer recognized him. There's a picture Carol took at that moment. The moment that the young boy burst into tears while holding in his hands the face of his small and terrified pet. It wasn't the reunion we expected. It wasn't the reunion all of us had hoped for. The family looked forlorn as they gently led their dog away.

The calendar marked the arrival of Mardi Gras, and for the residents who had returned, the celebration brought some semblance of life back to New Orleans. In early 2006, the city was just barely starting to come back, and the upcoming carnival season was fodder for much debate. In the daily newspaper, the *Times-Picayune*, people weighed in on both sides of the controversy, some voicing concern that there was little to celebrate and others insisting it would provide a much-needed emotional lift to the wounded city. Bead stores sprung up, and I was eager to do something as mundane as shop for souvenirs. Those beads brought a lot of color to our lives in the sepia-toned disaster zone, and most everyone had a pile of them draped on their rearview mirror or hanging off the neck rests in their trucks and SUVs. Even some of our animals wore them. I had longed to wear Mardi Gras beads, see Lake Pontchartrain, drink chicory-laced coffee, and stroll through the French Quarter. The feelings I had for New Orleans ran deep. I couldn't explain it. Like I said, it came from books and a movie. Every chance I got I told people how happy I was to be there. They would all respond the same way: "You should have seen her before the storm."

Mardi Gras 2006 went on as planned. A bunch of us decided to take a rare night off and head downtown to the Muses parade on St. Charles. Most of us had never been to Mardi Gras, and we were excited to celebrate our newfound home. We sat outside an outdoor bar and watched as the streets gradually filled with people. It was nighttime, and families with kids strolled by as we anxiously awaited the parade from our perch in the patio area of the bar. The street pulsed like a bass riff. Soon the music started, and the police escorts cruised by. People were dancing and swaying in the street. We watched the marching bands waltz by in their brightly colored, ornate uniforms, their instruments gleaming in the night. One man walked the side of the parade, and I heard him say, "Welcome home, everyone, welcome home." The floats were lavishly decorated and the revelers hung over their sides and laughed and danced while throwing beads to hundreds of outstretched hands. Our smiles wide, our arms outstretched, we begged for those "throws" and placed the beads bright with promise around our necks. Carol took pictures and, in a rare instance, found herself in the center of one.

Anderson Cooper was coming to town to cover the first post-Katrina Mardi Gras celebration. An animal lover, he wanted to do a story on the animal rescue effort, and rumor had it he was going to visit Celebration Station. The Best Friends folks, who were the logistics coordinators for everything that happened at Celebration Station, were very excited at the possibilities a visit by the Silver Fox himself could bring. The initial shock of Katrina had worn off for most of America, and disaster fatigue had set in. A national story by a big, major-network star would raise public awareness. Maybe his visit would spur more action and generate a fresh wave of donations and adoptive homes for the animals.

The day Anderson Cooper arrived was cold and overcast. Everyone worked to tidy up the place. We were putting our best foot forward; his visit marked the first time the mainstream media had paid any attention to the animal rescue efforts. It was validating. We were newsworthy. The caravan of vehicles signaling Anderson's arrival was long and late, and all of us clamored for a look at him. I had to figure out a way to get to him because this was an opportunity to get some attention focused on the animal situation in Waveland. Best Friends was making every effort to ensure he wasn't bombarded, but Barb, the Best Friends media manager, knew what I had been up against in Mississippi. After a brief chat, she agreed to let me speak with Anderson if the opportunity presented itself. It was up to me to ensure it did.

He walked in the door with a long trail of photographers and people with clipboards in his wake. His blue eyes scanned the room and lit up when he was approached by one of the Best Friends staff. He was much shorter than I expected, and had an easy, calm, competent presence that made him instantly likable. A crowd followed him wherever he went. He spent a few minutes with Red, a pit bull who had been hit by a car in the early days after the storm. A homeless man had found him lying near death on the street. Both of them struggled on the streets until an ARNO volunteer heard about them and brought Red to Hound Zero. He had emergency surgery, but both of his hind legs were paralyzed. A donated cart to secure his back legs allowed him to walk around the facility, and when it was time for him to rest, he would lie in the middle of the first floor beneath the disco ball that still hung from the ceiling. But Red never sat still for long, and there was always someone who wanted to play with him. Watching folks throw a ball for Red brought smiles and tears from the audience as Red ran as fast as he could on two good front legs while dragging his entire rear quarters behind him. Anderson stroked Red's coat while one of Red's handlers recounted his story. Watching him touch Red like that, I knew all I needed to know about Anderson Cooper. He may have come looking for a unique angle on the Katrina story, but the guy really cared about animals. There was no disputing that.

I watched the people nearest to him and tried to figure out who might be the best person to approach. There were so many people in his entourage that getting to him one-on-one would be impossible without a facilitator. I guess that was the point.

When I got the chance, I pulled aside the guy Anderson spoke with the most and asked if I could have a minute. As luck would have it, he was Anderson's personal manager. I explained that I had been working in Waveland, Mississippi, and that things there were awful for the animals. I had heard that Anderson's next stop was Waveland. His manager told me they were on a really tight schedule, but he'd see what he could do.

As the tour began to wind down, his manager pulled Cooper aside, whispered in his ear, and looked my way. Anderson approached me, put an arm around my shoulder, and we slowly walked together for a few minutes. I knew I had too little time, so I quickly described what had been happening in Waveland. I told him we needed help exposing what was happening at the shelter. He listened to what I had to say, asked me a few questions, stood for a picture a friend wanted to take of us, shook my hand, and walked away. He reported that night on the evening news; the ghost town of Waveland was the back-drop. I watched with the others, huddled around a small TV. Helplessly hoping he'd throw us a bone. He never mentioned the shelter or the animals.

I was beginning to feel very much alone in my fight for the animals of Waveland.

The next few days were a blur. I was reluctant to venture across the Mississippi state line, so I stayed put. The contact who had a boyfriend on the Waveland police force called to tell me there was deep dissension within the ranks. A few cops had nick-named me "the little animal-sider," and secretly championed my work. They thought it was high time someone kicked some ass about the shelter and what was happening to their community's animals. In the minority, and out of fear they'd lose their jobs, they kept quiet. And, again and again, people told me I had enemies who would have been happy to see me "dead in a culvert on a backcountry road." My mind conjured images of the cars of civil rights workers being pulled from ponds in the not-so-distant past. The voices expressing concern for my safety grew.

Regardless of which side the police were on, it was made clear that no one would do a damn thing. Even when unspoken, resentment and bitterness ran deep across a cultural divide: northerners, or "Yankees," thought they were superior, the Civil War, a not-so-distant reminder of northern aggression. They didn't know a damn about how things were in the South. When I was told that the members of the force who loved animals but wouldn't dare speak out because they could lose their jobs, I was shocked. It was crazy enough to think I could be hurt because I was trying to save dogs and cats, but to be told the police were silenced because of fear was outrageous. At first, it had all seemed so ridiculous to me, but folks in Mississippi did not like others meddling in their business. I was an outsider. Hell, people from the next county were considered outsiders. People couldn't decide whether I was crazy or just plain stupid.

Pissed and stubborn was what I was. I had witnessed too much apathy and cruelty. I had no choice but to continue to fight for the animals. And I wasn't alone. Animals in communities like Waveland had been neglected and mistreated for decades. When the waves of Katrina receded, they exposed a truth that many in this community had known and could do little about for years. Now that people from other parts of the country had arrived in the Deep South and witnessed the brutality, there was no turning back. I wasn't going anywhere until the animals were safe and something changed in Waveland. There simply was no choice.

For two weeks, I worked from Celebration Station. All attempts to determine if there was a warrant for my arrest proved futile. Chase and I spoke daily, his wife answering the calls. Roberta was still simmering, monitoring her staff to assure that no one broke the code of silence. I feared she'd take her anger out on the animals. She believed I was the root of all of their troubles. Staying away was the safest and hardest thing I'd ever had to do.

The days flew by. That's what happens when you find something that yanks you out of bed every morning like a fish on a hook. I struggled to fall asleep at night and couldn't wait to get up and do it all again the next day. Trixie was thriving on the attention Carol and I gave her. We massaged her legs and encouraged her to walk. Every day she had her water therapy, and we hated to put her back in her little cage if we weren't going to be around for a few hours.

Red was getting more and more comfortable in his wheelchair, and some were trying to find a rescue that could take him. It's not easy finding a home for a paralyzed pit bull, but we managed. The day Red left, we all signed his crate with a black permanent marker and sent messages to the folks in Texas who were taking him in. We wanted them to know how special he was. Most of us cried as he was loaded into the truck. Red had become a symbol of survival and hope for us all.

With each new day, I was growing more and more impatient to get back to Waveland. People were starting to trickle back into that community, and the word was getting around that Animal Rescue Front was on a crusade to change the way animals were being treated in their shelter. As people returned, the pressure started to grow. Forums were springing up in the local papers. Everyone had an opinion, and most were not supportive. I heard stories of corruption and misappropriation of funds. Tommy Longo, the mayor, was repeatedly trashed, as was I. Some supported the spotlight I was shining in dark corners, but others just wanted the "outsiders" to mind our business and go back to where we came from. To say we were controversial was an understatement. But my efforts to network with local community members finally started to bear fruit. Word of mouth put me in touch with Peg, who had grown up in Waveland and still had family there. But a bad marriage to a violent man forced her to take her two children and flee as far from Mississippi as she could get. Peg and I spoke every night by phone, and she helped me understand the obstacles and attitudes I was facing in Hancock County. She told me the word on the street was that I had made a lot of powerful people unhappy. If I was going to venture back, she cautioned I would need protection.

"I have someone who knows some people who ride motorcycles," she said.

"They'd scare you half to death to look at them, but they don't like people who hurt animals."

A local group of business owners in Hancock County supported the shelter and its animals. Many were from the Bay St. Louis area, and was as hard hit as Waveland, so home phone and business numbers were not in service. I was able to get the cell phone number of one member, and one night I called her. We spoke for about forty-five minutes, and I told her what we had been dealing with since finding the shelter in early October. I asked if we could work together to make things better for the animals. She said it would take a few days to speak with others from their group because all of their records and computer equipment had been destroyed by the storm. Getting ahold of folks would be tough. Many had lost their homes. Phones rang unanswered, and because some members of the group had evacuated to other states, no one knew where they were. When we hung up, I was hopeful. Maybe I could muster enough allies to topple Roberta's evil little empire after all.

Late the next night, my phone rang. It was the woman I had spoken to less than twenty-four hours before.

"We don't want to get involved," she said. Then she hung up. Wait. What?

I stood there looking at my phone. They don't want to get involved? How in the hell could they *not* get involved? My shock quickly gave way to fury before my rage plummeted into despair when I realized the local people wouldn't even work with us. I needed to get back there. But my friends refused to let me drive into Mississippi alone. It started to feel like a poorly written B-grade movie. Police, threats, rumors, corruption—what in the hell was going on? I started to question how much danger I was really in. I entertained the thought that it was all a joke. I can't possibly be in danger. That's insane. I called Connie in Washington. "Maybe it's best if you listen to the ones that know what's really going on," she said. "Listen to the folks who have lived it all their lives."

I started to take it seriously. I decided it was best left to the people who had lived there and knew the political and cultural structures. When a trio of Canadian women made plans to pick up a few dogs at the Humane Society in Gulfport, they offered me a ride. Even if it did turn out I was a fugitive on the lam, they joked, at least I'd have the cover of a car with Canadian plates. Michelle would meet at HSSM to start planning our next trans-port of animals. I'd stay at her home and use her vehicle if I needed to drive anywhere.

That night I called Peg and told her I was leaving New Orleans the next morning. I gave her the vehicle description and plate number and the date and time we would be leaving Celebration Station. We estimated my arrival in Gulfport. She said she'd call back in a few hours. Like clockwork, a few hours later, my phone rang. Peg had heard back from her biker friends.

"You will not know you are being followed. These guys are very good at what they do," she said. "Only one of them is allowed to make contact with you, and it will only be in the case of an emergency. If you are approached by a man with a goatee and ponytail who tells you his name is Arn, and he tells you we have to go now, and those are the exact words he will use, you do not pack your bags, you don't question him. You go." I thanked her, and she wished me luck.

That night I lay awake, and the familiar sounds of bedtime consoled me, but sleep evaded. It was very likely to be the last time I would be rescuing animals in New Orleans, and a tear fell from my eye. And while I was filled with excitement to be going back to Mississippi, there was profound sadness at leaving the safe embrace of our community home. The love, the laughter, my comfortable air mattress next to Carol and Trixie were home like I had never known. I fit in, belonged, felt needed, even treasured, surrounded by people who had walked away from everything and packed on this city's heartbreak. The selfless courage and bravery I had witnessed firsthand; the honor I felt being amongst such heroes.

And while the anticipation of what tomorrow would bring made my heart beat harder in my chest, I mourned the closing of this chapter in my life. Mississippi was where I was needed. It was where I was meant to be. Through all of the tragedy, I had witnessed the inspiration that sustained me as I considered what lay ahead.

Chapter Ten

Mississippi Barking

I was never once afraid. Hesitant, maybe, but not scared. Not amongst the soldiers with their rifles or the dogs with their fear. But after weeks of hearing horror stories and leaving the safety of New Orleans, I started feeling a little paranoid. If there were people I had pissed off that wanted me to shut up, I'd deal with it. After all, I had a motorcycle gang watching my back. What could possibly happen?

I had become close with the small Canadian contingent of women led by Meg Brubacher. Meg had lost her job the week Katrina hit the Gulf Coast. Having too much time on her hands, she continually watched CNN from her home in Guelph, Ontario. Having once lived in Louisiana and Mississippi, she was intimately familiar with the gravity of the homeless pet situation in those states. She went to the Gulf Coast four times. Her first trip to Louisiana was nine days after the storm.

Traci Dawson was home one night watching the local news when a story ran about a Guelph woman who had traveled south to help the animals of Katrina. Traci, a longtime animal rescuer herself, took the plea personally, and when Meg gave her phone number over the air and said through tears that the animals needed a lot of help, she knew she had to go. Phones rang, plans were made. Meg's longtime friend Kathleen Dube joined them. I met all three at Celebration Station. We became bonded in the way I imagined soldiers at war might do. They were headed home to Ontario and scheduled to pick up four dogs in Gulfport for the trip. They offered me a ride.

After a long round of tearful goodbyes, we headed east. It was a sun-filled but chilly early spring day. I was in the backseat feeling a mix of apprehension and anticipation as we pulled out of the Celebration Station parking lot. Many of our friends stood together and watched us drive away. There's a picture I saw years later, my left hand hanging out the rear passenger window, my fingers flashing a peace sign.

Destination: Gulfport. The trip felt longer this time. I found myself frequently looking over my shoulder. Paranoia had joined me for the ride. When we passed a Mississippi State Trooper, I held my breath. My mind was playing tricks on me. I'd imagined we'd get pulled over and have to show identification. I'd be handcuffed and led away. I'd never be seen or heard from again.

Scenes from *Mississippi Burning* played in my head. I'd be found dead in a culvert on some remote and rutted road. The other scene in my mind was of a big media circus that would ensue, and the shelter would finally be exposed for what it was. That's the one I was hoping for. Either way, I was nervous. All I wanted was for the animals to be safe. Maybe my outsider status emboldened my unique position. Maybe it condemned it. I was a Yankee, after all. Either way, I wasn't going away. I could not un-see what I had seen. I could not stop caring.

Before leaving New Orleans, Jess Higgins and Cadi Schiffer had made me a gift. We had a dog tag engraver, and Cadi had made me two tags. One was a red heart-shaped tag that read "The Little Animal Sider" on one side and "Waveland, MS.

2005–2006 Never Again" on the back. The second was a bronze dog bone-shaped pendant that read "Hurricane Katrina Animal Rescue 2005–2006" with the reverse reading "Mississippi's Angel (& Avenger)." I held those tags in my hand the entire way and didn't take them off my neck for years. They were a badge of honor. The highest recognition I could receive from my friends. I believed they'd bring me luck and keep me safe and remind me that I would never be alone.

This would be my first trip to the new Humane Society of South Mississippi. Located out on I-49 just minutes from the coast, it was a significant improvement over the army bunker by the sewage treatment plant that served as the shelter for years. As we drove, I didn't see one motorcycle. We pulled into the large parking lot that had a welcoming entryway to the lobby. The lobby was cheerful and bright, with a small retail store selling animal-related gear and gifts. It was shiny and clean. After spending days in the bunker, this was such a welcome sight. The animals of Harrison County, Mississippi, had a new home. And what a home it was!

Michelle was paged and met us out front. Together we loaded four Gulfport dogs into the back of the Suburban. Those lucky ones were headed to Canada. I couldn't help but feel like I was being watched. Or was I paranoid? I asked myself. Occasionally I'd look behind my back. Behind the parking lot was a large area that had been cleared for a planned community dog park. No motorcycles. No men with ponytails. I was losing it.

My Canadian friends and I said our goodbyes within the hour, and Michelle asked if I wanted to run some errands with her. She had to go to the post office and make a few other stops.

Maybe we could grab a sandwich while we were out? I said sure, and we left.

The day had become steamy and bright. I hadn't been to Gulfport since December, and now in early March, it was coming back to life. I tried to relax while Michelle drove. I saw one motorcycle. He paid no attention to us.

The instructions Peg had given me kept sounding in my head. I was sure once again it was all just a bunch of crap—that the emotional high wire so many of us were living had blown any remnants of sanity right out the window. But later that night, back at Michelle's, Peg called and told me about my day. She knew every stop we had made. I was incredulous. The guys really were watching me.

My days in Gulfport were spent at the shelter, my nights at Michelle's home, with about thirty kittens. Her home had become an extension of the shelter. There were litters of kittens and a few special needs cats that lived with them. It was a luxury to be in a real bed. We had AC. I grew close to her kids, and at night we'd watch TV together. Little did I know that Peg's cousin slept outside Michelle's house every night I was there. He took this very seriously. Not once did I see him.

Between planning transports out of Gulfport and trying to get the media involved in pressuring city officials to deal with Waveland's situation, I kept busy. Letter-writing campaigns had started, and people from around the United States wrote letters voicing their concerns. The board of aldermen began to succumb to the pressure. The negative publicity had finally gotten their attention. I had been put in touch with one alderman who was genuinely concerned about the shelter—off the record, of course. We had a long talk late one night. He wanted to help but was outnumbered. The other alderman didn't care at all about the animal shelter, he said.

But things were starting to change. A public meeting was scheduled with the mayor and the aldermen, and I notified every media outlet on the Mississippi Gulf Coast. Al Showers, a local reporter from WLOX, had taken an interest in the shelter, and he said he'd be there. A reporter from the *Sun Herald*, the local paper in Biloxi, would be there too. I reached out to as many Waveland citizens as I could, and In Defense of Animals sent a representative who had photos proving conditions at the shelter were abhorrent and the neglect of the animals pervasive.

And the morning of the meeting, the call came.

Tommy Longo, the mayor, was requesting a closed-door meeting with me.

I wanted to decline. It was March 2006, and for five months, I had been trying to engage someone—anyone, anywhere—who could do something to address the situation at the animal shelter. Now, a media deluge was set to descend at the board of aldermen's meeting, and he wanted to talk. I didn't want to meet with him. I wanted to show up at the meeting with the cameras and microphones picking up every sordid story and picture we could throw at them. Through an intermediary, who insisted I had to meet with him, I agreed to a meeting for the following day.

For the first time, I was scared.

The rumored threats and covert activities we had engaged in made me feel I was putting myself at risk. And all that I'd heard about corruption and cronyism and the hatred for outsiders only fueled my fear. The online threads of public forums were terrifying. Folks mentioned stories from years past about donations for the shelter being circumvented to another of the city's needs. Whether they were rumors or not, the sheer number of stories made me feel very uneasy. Michelle insisted on going with me. She was intimately familiar with the hatred my presence generated. There was no way in hell she'd let me walk in there alone. I called Peg that night and told her what was going on. She assured me we wouldn't be alone.

That night Michelle and I picked up some takeout and brought it back to her house for the kids. We all watched TV in her large living room, barely saying a word about the next day. That night I didn't sleep well. Michelle didn't either.

The meeting at the mayor's office was set for 2:00 p.m. Michelle and I went to HSSM and kept ourselves busy—business as usual. But the occasional glances between us couldn't hide our anxiety. We had been invited into the lion's den and accepted the invitation. When it came time to head to Waveland, my fear shot through the roof.

In Diamondhead, Mississippi, we turned off the I-10 to get gas and something to drink. We pulled into an open bay at a gas station right off the exit, and a pickup truck pulled into the bay opposite us. I don't know what it was about that truck, but I noticed. Michelle started pumping gas while I walked into the store to grab a drink for the two of us, and as I walked back to her car, she was topping off the tank. The man driving the pickup truck had his back to me as he pumped gas, but his passenger looked my way. As I got closer, he lowered his sunglasses so I could see his eyes. He smiled at me in a way that told me all I needed to know. He was the guy that had been sleeping in front of Michelle's. He was the biker who followed my every move—Peg's cousin, my guardian angel, the scary guy who loved animals. And at that moment, I knew I'd be OK.

Waveland's City Hall was swept away by Katrina. All that remained of the quaint, historic building were the front stairs and the flagpole. The mayor's office was now in a FEMA trailer by the railroad tracks. As were the fire and police departments. When I got out of Michelle's car that bright and sunny March afternoon, it was the first time I'd taken a step in Waveland since before the rescue of the Waveland Four. We were asked to take a seat when we introduced ourselves, and it wasn't lost on me that the woman behind the desk scowled when she did so. A few minutes later, my hands shaking, we were escorted into an office in the government-issued trailer. The office was large and dark, the windows small and curtained.

Mayor Longo stood and, from behind his desk, extended his hand. He had an easy smile and asked us to "please take a seat." I wanted to hate him. I did hate him. And then we talked, and I couldn't hate him. The consummate politician, he was welcoming and smiled frequently. He had an ease about him, and the conversation was civil, sometimes even jovial. He asked me what it would take to "fix" his shelter, and I told him he had to fire the entire staff. I told him the things I had witnessed and the stories I had been told of the nightmare that was his shelter. The countless animals neglected, killed, tortured, and sold out the backdoor to friends and friends of friends. The dogfighting animal control officers. He refused to believe that someone like Larry could have done some of the things I had heard. "The staff lost everything," he told me. "They are suffering from post-traumatic stress disorder." That was his defense of them. "This has been going on for years, Mayor Longo," I said. "Well before Katrina."

An hour and a half later, we had reached an agreement. The staff would stay, but they had to work with us. Michelle would begin a full-time position overseeing shelter operations. The city was unable to pay her salary, so I had to figure out how we could make that happen. Mayor Longo gave us his full support to resume transports. How we would continue to pay for them was another matter. The city had no money, we were told. He'd offer cooperation, but the funding had to come from elsewhere. I asked him for his personal cell phone number and said that he had to answer my call no matter what time of day or night, or our agreement was off. He promised he would. We agreed that we would show a united front at the aldermen's meeting that night and announce that change was coming to the Waveland Animal Shelter.

In the coming weeks, Mayor Longo and I would attempt to secure funding for a brand-new shelter in Waveland. I talked with people at the Humane Society of the United States about dispersing some of the donations they had received, a purported $34 million. Still, I was a lone ranger and not yet a federally recognized charity. They weren't interested in what was taking place at the hardest hit shelter on the Gulf Coast.

As Michelle and I left the FEMA trailer that day, we unexpectedly walked right into Roberta. She was looking at the ground as she approached the front stairs. Her face startled then frowned when her eyes met mine. But there was nothing she could do to me now. I grinned.

I surprised even myself when I gave her a hug.

The public meeting with the mayor and the aldermen was the turning point in a long and sad history for the animals of Hancock County, Mississippi. Shortly after we met with the mayor, Best Friends in Utah stepped up. Again. A few nights later, I received a call from a woman named Laura Bradshaw. Laura ran a sanctuary for disabled or paralyzed animals not far from Best Friends in Kanab, Utah. She had a good friend there,

Amy Hogg. Laura had heard about ARF through Laurel Ley, a key coordinator at Celebration Station who had left her home in Florida and was living in an RV in the parking lot. They asked how they could help with the situation in Waveland. I recapped the meeting with the mayor and a few days later Amy called to tell me the stunning news: Best Friends would fund our entire operation for the next three months. For the next three months, using donations from the public for Hurricane Katrina animal rescue relief work, Michelle received a salary and went to the Waveland Animal Shelter every day. With the funding, we hired a part-time veterinary technician. With a trained tech and money for medicine and vaccines every animal entering the shelter would be vaccinated and wormed. For the very first time, the Waveland animals would get what they needed to get the best possible start to their lives and keep them healthy prior to transport.

The money from Best Friends proved helpful in other ways. Medical emergencies would be covered in full—any and all. We had a large litter of puppies that came down with parvo, a particularly deadly disease. In those days, if a litter was even suspected of having parvo they were immediately put down. Michelle and I were able to take them to an emergency veterinary hospital where they were aggressively treated and survived. Mange and infections, sprains and wounds—if they could be treated by our vet tech, they were. If they couldn't, we could bring them to a vet clinic and not worry about the bills.

The rental vans and gas receipts would be covered for every transport. And transport them we did. William, a local resident and our vet tech, and his then-partner, Dorty, drove all over the United States to get the Waveland animals to safety. Having never left the state before Katrina, he jumped at the opportunity. We sent transports to Washington State, Idaho,

Colorado, California, Arizona, Maryland, North Carolina, New England, and his favorite trip: upstate New York and Niagara Falls. He took that trip many times, and each time he went to see the Falls.

What began as an extremely contentious relationship with Roberta gradually found its way to a mutual understanding that we were stuck with each other and might as well make the best of it. And slowly over time, she started to come around. I no longer dreaded walking into the shelter. Some days she even smiled and interacted with me in a casual and lighthearted way. Record-keeping began, and she would occasionally ask Michelle and William for guidance or opinion. If an animal needed ongoing medicine, she would make sure it got done, and a small bulletin board hung on a wall and was filled with posters from local residents looking for their lost animals. And when it came time to load up for transport, Michelle and I were no longer doing all of the work. Roberta was right there, in the vehicle, making sure everyone was loaded safely.

The funding would pay my expenses as well. I would be in Waveland for at least one week every month for the next three months, overseeing what I hoped would become the complete turnaround of the Waveland Animal Shelter.

It wasn't perfect. One morning on our way to the Louis Armstrong New Orleans International Airport, Michelle and I decided to unexpectedly stop by the shelter. I walked into an overfull kennel and not a single staff member was in sight. The cages were disgusting, filled with urine and dried feces. It was clear they had not been cleaned since the day before, and it was 9:30 in the morning. The staff came in at 8:00 a.m. I walked down the rows and peered in the cages, my anger building. There was a cage of feces-covered puppies cowering and shaking all huddled in the corner, clearly terrified of their circumstances. I pulled out my phone and took pictures. It was all I could do to not scream or break down and cry. We went into the FEMA trailer where the staff was hanging out, and the collective looks of surprise on their faces revealed they knew they'd been caught. I asked why the cages weren't clean at 9:30 in the morning. Blank stares glared back at me. Then, slowly, Chase and Tori stood up and walked to the kennels. It was a showdown: a power play. Roberta looked away and busied herself with paperwork.

There was no explanation. No words were exchanged. I called the mayor and told him what we had walked in on. He told me he'd look into it immediately. The puppies that had been so afraid and suffering in their own waste got sick and had to be put down. They were beautiful, fluffy little white babies who couldn't care for themselves. No one cared to spay their mother, and no one cared enough to keep them out of a condemned shelter. Thankfully Michelle and William took care of them as they passed. Years later, I can still see those puppies' faces, the whites of their eyes looking up at me from feces encrusted faces. I am haunted still that we couldn't save them.

Chubby had dogs in the bed of his pickup and a Glock on his front seat. He made sure I knew who would win the argument. It was May, and the heat was bearing down on Waveland and I was on my monthly trip to the coast. Michelle and I were in the office when Chubby—the Waveland animal control officer, pit-bull breeder, and alleged dogfighter—pulled into the parking lot. This morning he had found two strays running the streets. They were in cages in the back. When he pulled up, Michelle and I went out to greet him. I didn't want them to step one foot in the shelter, and I was headed to New Orleans shortly to take some animals who would be leaving on a Best Friends transport that night. The shelter was very full, and Michelle and I were desperate to ease the burden that day. I wanted the dogs to go straight to my vehicle.

From the start, Chubby and I had a tenuous relationship. I was cordial and kind, but it was a guise and a challenge. I needed him to like me to get his cooperation. The constant flirtations he attempted to engage me with made my stomach turn. But for the sake of the animals, I just laughed them off. For the most part, it had worked.

That day my luck ran out.

Maybe it was because I felt emboldened by my support from the mayor, or perhaps it was the tremendous stress I had been under for months, but an argument ensued. Chubby was pissed. His job was to put them in the shelter. Mine was to take them out. He went to the cab of his truck and played the tiebreaker.

Michelle grabbed my arm and turned me towards the office stairs. Once inside, she called the police. We waited in the office while Chubby paced in the parking lot. He was on the phone and I could hear his loud voice from inside. About twenty minutes went by before a police cruiser arrived. There were two officers, one male, one female. Michelle and I stepped outside. The female officer approached first, her hands hooked on either side of her heavy leather belt, a look of disinterested hostility on her face. I held out my hand to introduce myself. She looked me dead in the eye and said, "I know who you are." She did not shake my hand.

It only got worse from there.

She asked Chubby what had happened and then listened to my version of events. They had little in common. The Glock in his hand didn't concern her, nor did my fear that he was going to use it. She asked me to just chalk it up to a "little misunder-standing." After a few minutes, they looked at me, and Michelle then got in their cruiser and drove away. Chubby got into his vehicle and peeled out of the parking lot. The dogs were taken out back and placed in cages. They weren't going to be able to leave right away and I was scared to death they'd kill them to spite me. And I knew I'd never call the police for help again.

Chapter Eleven

Honey Bear Belle

My life had been a nomadic one. I was kicked out of my home at eighteen and bounced around the greater Boston area for years. Never living anywhere long, I went through roommates and relationships at a steady clip. The longest I lived in any one place was a loft I owned in Cambridge, Massachusetts, but settled in sobriety and after seven years of living in the inner city, I wanted a large yard for my dogs, and the quiet of western Massachusetts was very appealing. As were the home prices. Growing roots had eluded me, but the antique Cape built in 1790 felt perfect. I'd heat with wood, and my dogs had twelve acres of land. A small pond and stream provided hours of enjoyment as, each spring, I watched the Mallards begin a new brood. A lone beaver appeared one year, and my neighbors laughed when I welcomed his arrival. "You won't be happy when he floods your yard," one laughingly remarked. But the pond proved too much of a challenge, and much to my dismay, the beaver moved on.

My information technology career had been a relatively lucrative one, but I had little to show for it. Five years of unemployment after 9/11 had depleted my savings account. Eventually, the home on twelve acres proved to be far too secluded from family and friends, and on long winter nights, the darkness and cold were very isolating. Striking a balance for solitude and community had become a struggle, and the comfort of a wood stove and the wildlife I shared my world with, no longer emotionally sustained me. The summer of Katrina, I moved to Cape Cod, which reunited me with community and family, but finding suitable permanent housing with three dogs was tough in the tourist-fed and second-home economy. I was in our third living situation in six months when my uncle's home on the bayside of North Eastham was offered to us, so Macy, Demi, Honey Bear, and I moved in.

Honey Bear's heartworm treatment was successful, but she had to be kept calm for three months for her battered heart to heal. The four of us settled into an easy rhythm of short walks along the sandy paths and quiet nights when the darkness fell. I navigated the need to secure professional employment and continued the work in Waveland. The frequent trips back and forth to the Gulf Coast were exhausting and kept me in a cultural and climate limbo. While the snow fell on Cape Cod, the heat rose in Mississippi. But it was perfect. I scheduled transports from my home office and kept daily contact with Michelle and William. The mayor and I spoke at least weekly, and he was pleased with the progress we were making.

I had been struggling with the decision to keep Honey Bear, but something inside kept my enthusiasm at bay. I had this sense that she didn't "belong" to me. I imagined her in a forever home with a single man—one without children, wife, or other dogs. I imagined the man would tell me he was "in love with her." That's what I wanted most for Honey Bear Belle. And as strange as it might sound, that was exactly what happened.

In March, and during the extended trip, when I had met with the mayor, my cell phone rang, and it was Penn. Penn was a good friend and local shipbuilder, the next town over. He had offered to take care of Honey while I traveled for ARF. One night Penn had stopped at the Chocolate Sparrow, a local Cape Cod coffeehouse, when Woody, a friend of his, happened to walk by. Honey Bear was sitting upright in the passenger seat of Penn's truck looking longingly at the café. Woody's first thought he later told me was, "What is Penn doing with my dog?" Woody hadn't had a dog in over three years. His last dog had died tragically in front of him. A lifelong doggie dad he had sworn he'd never have another.

"Hey, Penn! Everything OK," I asked.

"I am standing here with my friend Woody," he said. "And he just saw Honey Bear out front in my truck. He wants to ask you some questions about her. He says he's in love with her."

Boom.

"Put him on," I said.

"Hi Chris, my name is Woody. I'm the guy who's in love with your dog. By any chance, does she need a home?"

Why yes, she did, I thought to myself. To a man. Single. No family or kids. Who was in love with her.

Woody.

A few weeks later, on a weekday evening, Woody pulled into the lot of the Hole-in-One-Donut Shoppe in a 1982 Mercedes-Benz sedan that ran on vegetable oil. He followed me down the discreet bayside sandy path that led to my uncle's house. When we got there, we sat in the living room, Honey between us on her bed on the floor. I let Woody talk. Softly defiant, he couldn't possibly convince me he was the one for her. If I found something wrong with him, I could say I tried and just keep her. A part of me simply didn't want to let her go. He had no girlfriend and was a caretaker for a friend's home on a kettle pond in Orleans. He had his own house-painting business and had grown up on Cape Cod. Throughout his life, he'd always had dogs. But three years prior, he was sitting in his kitchen one summer day, the half-screen, half-solid porch door closed and, suddenly, his dog leaped to her feet and jumped right through the door screen. Whether it was a fox or a rabbit, he'd never know, but she gave chase right into the road and was hit by a car. She was three years old. Woody was certain he'd never have another dog.

"All of my friends have dogs," he told me.

"They've been bugging me for a long time to get another. I've had them my entire life. I know where every one of them is buried. But I swore I'd never get another dog. And when I saw Honey, there was just something about her. And that crazy thought entered my mind that she was 'my dog.'"

At that exact moment, Honey got up from her place on the floor. She crawled up onto my lap, something she had never done before, and rested her precious golden redhead on my shoulder. We stayed that way for at least a minute, the silence growing between us. My heart beat fast. Then she got down and walked over to Woody. I didn't know it at the time, but it was her way of thanking me. Of telling me she was OK now—that I had found her person.

And I had.

Honey Bear belonged to Woody as much as he belonged to her. And it took a hurricane and 1,600 miles to bring them together. Honey Bear left that night in the front seat of that beat-up Benz.

After they left, I lay awake, looking at the ceiling in the darkness. Honey Bear had survived the worst natural disaster in United States history. Somehow, she ended up at a hazardous shelter where very few survived. I'd found her and took her to New Orleans, where she was seen by a veterinarian and diagnosed with a disease that left untreated would have delivered a horrible death. She stayed with me in the SUV, and in the apartment on Coliseum, where pieces of the living room ceiling were falling in on us as we slept.

She drove with me the long way home.

But this night I had found her home. The home she was always meant to have. Honey Bear belonged to a brokenhearted man who had given up on ever sharing his life again with another dog—1,600 miles between them. Mississippi to Massachusetts. The connection they had was as if they'd known each other forever. He was her person. I lay in bed, thinking about what had happened since she came into my life. The faces of all the dogs and puppies, cats, and kittens that had crossed my path since that October day when I drove to a place I'd never been or could not have imagined—1,600 miles from a familiar face or a friendly hand. It was then I knew what I'd found. If Honey Bear belonged to Woody, then the others belonged to someone too. I'd build a website and post their pictures. I'd call prospective adopters and reach out to friends of friends. If it meant driving them all over the country, I'd find their people.

And through finding them, I found me.

Chapter Twelve

Boots

With the funding from Best Friends, the entire focus of my work was Waveland, and Gulfport became my second home. By the summer of 2006, I was going back and forth to the area every few weeks. It was exhausting but inevitable. Hands-on was the best way to enact change at the Waveland shelter. Staying at home felt impossible with so much at stake. I was restless and discontent. The only thing that made me happy was being in Mississippi and helping the animals.

I'd leave my home for the 3:00 a.m. bus to Logan Airport in Boston. With no direct flights to Gulfport, I'd layover for an hour or two in Atlanta before boarding a plane to Gulfport. It was on one of these trips that I met a woman named Laura.

The plane was small, with single seats on either side. Halfway through the flight from Atlanta, I grew restless and got up to stretch my legs. On the return to my seat, I stalled in aisle five while the flight attendant served drinks. As I enjoyed the upright moment, a woman at my back asked me about the shirt I was wearing. It was a gift from a friend who had been at an antiwar demonstration in New York City days before, and the back of the shirt had an image of the boots of fallen American soldiers killed in the war in Iraq.

When I told her where I had gotten the shirt, my Boston accent, devoid of the letter "r," gave me away. She asked me why someone from Massachusetts was flying to Gulfport. "Animal rescue," I said. She started to look sad, and her eyes glistened with tears. And then she told me her story.

Her family, their dog, and their home had miraculously survived Katrina even though they lived only a few blocks inland from the Gulfport coast. The fence surrounding their property had been damaged, and their roof lost most of its shingles from the high winds. They hired workers to replace the temporary fence her husband had built for their dog, but the workers neglected to close the gate one day. Their dog, Chloe, wandered away.

"Do you know where she might have been taken?" she asked.

I asked for her phone number and gave her my email address. I knew some of the smaller organizations rescuing animals in the Gulfport area in the months after the hurricane. "Do you have a picture?" I asked. "I'll send you one," she said.

Shortly after, all the drinks served, I returned to my seat. I tried to read my book, but I couldn't forget the look in Laura's eyes. I went back to her aisle. "I want you to know that the people doing rescue in Gulfport were really incredible," I told her. "The chances are excellent Chloe was picked up and transported out of state where she would be adopted to another family." Laura appeared a bit relieved. "In the months after Katrina, the animals that survived the disaster were in high demand by the public," I assured her. I was cautiously optimistic that one of the rescuers had found her.

"We checked the shelter every day," she told me. "We called animal control, and the Public Works Department praying she hadn't been hit by a car. No one had any reports for a dog matching Chloe's description. After two months of looking, we gave up."

The plane landed in Gulfport, and Laura and I exited together. We hugged and parted ways. "Thank you for all you're doing for us," she said. I rented a vehicle and headed to HSSM. After my rounds of saying hello to everyone and seeing all the animals, I asked the staff if they remembered my friend Laura from the plane. "We remember her. Every day and sometimes more than once a day, she came in here looking for her dog," they said. "It was heartbreaking for us to see her and not be able to help."

I called Judy Clark of Triple R Pets in Illinois. Her group did most of the post-Katrina rescue in Gulfport and Jackson County, Mississippi. She asked me to send a picture of Chloe as soon as I could. In the meantime, she would talk to her local team, who had relocated to the area to continue saving animals.

The picture of Chloe came the next day in my email. I forwarded it to Judy. There wasn't anything particularly unusual about Chloe: she was an older black Lab, a white muzzle bordering her nose. She had no distinguishing marks or features. It would be next to impossible to identify her as one of the hundreds rescued from the streets of Gulfport in the months after the storm. But damn it, we would try. Judy asked me if Chloe had been wearing a collar or had a microchip. "Is there anything Laura can tell us about her that would make her stand out," she asked. I called Laura and asked, but there was nothing. No limp, no scars, no chip, just a friendly, white-muzzled older Lab. We never found Chloe. And while there were many Labs of all colors transported out of the area, no one would recall having transported a dog matching the photograph. I called Laura after a few days and broke the sad news. I tried to convince her that Chloe was safe somewhere. I hoped it was true.

For the next few days, I worked with Michelle to plan our next transport out of Gulfport. We had to assess everyone and determine who was qualified to travel. Paperwork had to be completed, and pictures had to be taken. The animals had to be healthy and current on their vaccinations. A few days after my last phone conversation with Laura, my phone rang. A previous ARF transport out of New Orleans had gone all the way to North Carolina, and the folks in North Carolina took eleven of the twelve dogs we had sent them. One was coming back— a female chocolate Lab originally from Waveland. Evidently, the folks in North Carolina didn't want any big breed dogs, as there were already too many of them in shelters there. The Lab had now survived Katrina, been moved from Waveland to New Orleans, spent two months in a clinic there, transported to North Carolina, turned down, and driven back to New Orleans. The clinic wanted to know what I wanted to do with her. I took a long shot. I called Laura.

When she answered the phone, I prefaced the call with a disclaimer: I didn't want her to feel any pressure about the now homeless Lab.

"I had an idea I'd like to run by you," I said. "A Waveland animal was returned on transport because they can't take in any larger dogs. It made me think of you guys."

"What kind of dog is it?" she asked.

"Well, that's why I thought of you. She's an adult chocolate Lab."

Laura was very interested and asked when they could meet her. I arranged the meeting for the next day, and her family took the one-hour trip to New Orleans to meet the Lab. A few hours had passed, and I found myself anxiously awaiting word.

Finally, my phone rang. It was Laura's number, and I hesitantly answered. I could immediately tell by the excitement in her voice when she explained that the car was a bit more crowded on the ride back to Gulfport because they had adopted "Abbie." That having met her, they instantly knew they wanted to adopt the big ole goofy Lab. Laura's voice skipped a bit when she thanked me for bringing some joy back into their lives. That Abbie was perfect and fit right into their family. And would Michelle and I please come and visit the next night and have dinner?

So, we did. The next night Michelle and I pulled up to a one-story brick house covered in a blue tarp. The front door opened and out bounced a welcoming and exuberant Lab, Abbie, looking like she'd lived there her whole life. Laura was right behind her, beaming, and quickly threw her arms around me in a hug that almost knocked me over. "Thank you so much," she told me softly. "Thank you."

Chapter Thirteen

Animal Rescue Front

With the support of the Waveland mayor and funding from Best Friends, Michelle resigned from HSSM and began working full-time at the Waveland Animal Shelter. The pet food storage room of the FEMA trailer became her new office and whether that was a result of it being the only option or the one furthest from the staff, and the smallest to boot, we didn't care. She'd be there five days a week, forty hours, and with a lot of luck, teaching the staff how to properly care for their community's animals. And, emboldened by my newfound support from the mayor, I laid down the edict that not one animal would be euthanized without my prior approval, or Michelle's, and even then it would only be considered for extreme aggression towards humans or life-threatening illness or injury that couldn't guarantee a certain quality of life.

William was at the shelter every day. Surrenders were commonplace. One family showed up with a laundry basket full of barely weaned puppies. When we asked where the mother was and why she wasn't fixed, the woman responded, "I wanted my children to experience the miracle of life." Little did she know had we not been there they would have been complicit in the death of every one of them.

We had to assume that none of those surrendered had received even the most minimal of care. They never came with medical records. William gave them their first vaccines, and their stools were checked for parasites. Those with skin issues were given topical medications, and all had a broad-spectrum wormer started. For the first time ever, the animals of Waveland were getting a fighting chance. Having medicine and vaccines was a miracle and lessened our anxiety about their health. Cataloging and identification systems were established, and each kennel had plastic sleeves hanging on their gates with the animal's name, identifying information, and medical records. Roberta and her staff went along with the changes because they were told they had to by the mayor. Most days, they begrudged our efforts and only did the bare minimum. Chase made efforts to better clean the cages, but when we saw him do it with animals inside, we let him know that would no longer be tolerated. We explained to him why that was. We hoped to lead by example, and that somehow compassion and common sense were transferable. Progress was slow. The others still spent most of the time in the office area while William, Michelle, and I spent most of ours with the animals. One day William told Michelle that he knew of a property Chase owned off the 603. He told us we had to go out there. On a day when we knew Chase probably wouldn't see us, we went.

We found five dogs chained to the chassis of broken-down and abandoned vehicles. All exposed to the intense southern sun. No water or food; their watchful eyes and low snarls kept us at a distance—that is, all but one whose long, thin teats brushed the barren ground, evidence of a mama dog having had far too many litters in her sad life. There were no puppies with her. She mustered a wiggle of a greeting when we approached. She was heartbreaking. Her bowls dirty and dry, we went to a faucet on the property and filled each one. We offered her water and loving hands and kind words—it was all we had. There were no legal protections that allowed for us to take them off the property. We would have been charged with stealing personal property and trespassing. There was a pen in the corner of the property, and we peeked over the wooden gate. Two wild boars were huddled together, trembling in the corner—large, wild boars, trembling at the sight of a human. You don't want to know why they were being held captive. I promise you, you don't.

The silence between us as we drove away was filled with hopelessness and despair. There was no one we could call. We decided we would bring them water and food. We didn't care if Chase found out. Within a few days they were gone.

Futile as our efforts sometimes seemed, we had to persist. The suffering of the animals fueled us. As long as Mayor Longo answered his phone and Best Friends paid the bills, we were in it for the long haul. We'd continue to petition the Humane Society of the United States for funding from the millions they took in for Hurricane Katrina relief. We would endure the daily dirty looks when we arrived for work. When we attended a small fundraiser for the local group that had refused to work with us, the air was noticeably chilly for a hot and humid summer day. Smirks and quiet conversations followed me wherever I went, the mayor at my side. I didn't want to care what people felt about me, but I'd be lying if I said it didn't hurt. All we wanted was something better for that community's animals. Something they should have had all along.

We had a lot of dogs get hit by cars. The first time I had to make the decision to put a dog to sleep came in the spring of 2006 when two little dogs, presumed to be sisters, got hit by a car. They were at a local vet who had recently reopened her hospital on Old Spanish Trail in Waveland. Less than twenty-four hours after they had been brought in, my phone rang. We were asked to come as soon as possible. When Michelle and I arrived, the vet gave me the sad news. One of the pups had more extensive injuries than the other. They couldn't get her pain under control, and she was suffering. I asked if I could go out back and see them. Both were lying together in a large kennel. Both lay on their sides. One appeared to be resting comfortably while the other whimpered. Her cries broke my heart. I didn't want her to die, but more than that, I didn't want her to suffer anymore. "I understand," I told the vet. "Do what you have to."

Although it was the right decision, it haunted me for days. It was a decision that has never come easy. When I first found Waveland, I secretly swore that not one animal would die on my watch. I'd do everything in my power to save them. What I had to learn was that some lives couldn't be saved. That sometimes, the most compassionate and humane thing to do was to ease one's suffering.

The summer of 2006 was a turning point of sorts, and little did I know that the hurricane on the coast would bring a personal storm to my life. By June, I was spending more time on Cape Cod, knowing that Michelle and William were handling things in Mississippi. I tried to relax. To take some time and integrate everything that had happened. Honey Bear and Buddy were in forever homes close to me on Cape Cod, and transports out of

Waveland continued. With Michelle overseeing things, I was much less worried about what was happening in the shelter. The funding from Best Friends kept the vaccines and medications stocked, and William knew enough about basic veterinary care that the animals were healthier and had a better chance of survival.

And I was alone.

In the quiet of an early June night, I had an anxiety attack. After months of constant activity and the emotionally charged life I had been leading, the silence closed in and consumed me. I panicked. I had to leave the house. I drove to the local ice cream shop because ice cream is what I thought I needed.

Earlier that day, a film crew came to Cape Cod to interview me for a Katrina animal rescue documentary. I should have been pumped. Proud. At the top of my game. I was being interviewed with some of the biggest names in the Katrina animal rescue story. But instead, I felt alone—disconnected, emotionally broken. The rain came down in sheets and splattered the windshield, creating colorful streaming rivers cast from the lights of the shop's sign. The colors looked beautiful in the raindrop's gleam. I sat in my car, watching people stream out the door, their cones clenched tight in fists. I stared. The ice cream wasn't what I needed. It wouldn't fill the hole inside me. It wouldn't wrap its arms around me. Ice cream wouldn't bring back the ones that died. My memories would never wash away. Not for a minute.

I pulled out of the parking lot and drove away. Images flooded my mind. That day I sat for the documentary crew for three hours. I told stories that were hard to hear: The pain of those left behind. The sadness of those who *left* behind. The sadness of a city. Remembering the emotional breakdown I had in Atlanta, where the freeway had been a jumble of tear-blurred signs. The dog lying broken in the Waveland Animal Shelter with no one there to comfort him while he passed.

Telling stories is a way of reliving them, and the stories I told that day hadn't been spoken to anyone. I halfheartedly hoped tomorrow it would all feel differently. I had been to the hell zone and back so many times, I no longer noticed the difference between the two. Down south, we were all in it together. Up here, I was all in it alone.

The film crew wanted to know how we dealt with the emotions. I told them we didn't have much time for that. Everyone was always on to the next thing. But when one of us did crumble from exhaustion or despair that we were all there to lift them up. That no one ventured out on their own. That the nights we all sat and ate at the long table at Celebration Station were the most comforting moments of most of our lives. We shared food, laughter, and tears. Maybe someone will see that documentary and be moved to follow the next disaster. Perhaps the telling of the stories will inspire someone to get up and go when the next levee breaks and the animals and the people are left to drown. If the earth opens up and swallows another city whole, maybe someone will hear. Maybe someone will care. Perhaps the experiences of Katrina will mean something to someone somewhere.

So many people have asked me how I did it: how do I go back and wade through the sadness again and again? I can't cry for one, I'd tell them. If I cried for one, I'd cry for them all. In moments alone or late at night, I see their little faces. Their suffering, their confusion, and their pain. My heart is broken in ways that I was just beginning to come to terms with. Remembering those animals we did save helps.

I think of the day I was visiting the sick bay unit at the HSSM. I was staying at the house of Tara's sister Cheryl during that trip, and early one morning, her son called to tell us a collie had just wandered into his garage and was in horrible shape. I dressed and drove to his home a few blocks away. When I arrived, I found the collie lying on a blanket Cheryl's son had put down for him. The poor dog's face looked like someone had thrown battery acid on it. It was red and raw and had large open sores. He helped me put the collie in the back of my vehicle, and I flew to HSSM. Later that day, the vet told me he had such a bad case of mange, mange that had gone untreated for so long it had begun to eat at the collie's face. Mange that either his owner did nothing about or as a result of living homeless on the streets. The treatment would take some time, and she hoped he would regain his eyesight, she said. A course of antibiotics would commence immediately.

The next day I visited my new collie ward with one of the contractors who was working to repair the shelter. His name was Mike. Mike was a nice guy with a big heart. I wanted him to know about the collie because I would be heading back to Boston soon, and I wanted someone to give him the attention and encouragement he would need to get well. I needed Mike to fill my shoes. Mike and I knelt down next to his cage, where he was resting comfortably. We opened the door to the cage, and Mike crawled a bit inside. His hand gently stroking the collie's coat, his whispered words of comfort made the collie's eyes close softly.

The next day Mike showed up at the shelter with a brand-new dog bed. He wanted the collie to be comfortable, he said. I hugged him with all my might. This man, a stranger, had assumed a bit of my burden. I felt relief that the collie would have someone visiting him and taking an interest. A few weeks later, the staff told me they had sent him to a collie rescue group in northern Louisiana. And a few months later they sent us an email and picture of "Charleston." He was magnificent in a full and merle-colored coat. His face was healed and resplendent. Charleston was posed as if for the winning picture in Best in Show contest.

By the summer of 2006, some semblance of life had returned to the Mississippi Gulf Coast. Most of the debris had been hauled away, and there were more recreational vehicles and FEMA trailers parked in driveways and on concrete slabs. Construction crews were busy framing out new homes and banging nails. A few businesses and restaurants had reopened. The fire station next to the shelter would never reopen, but the firemen and police had new FEMA trailers. Some days Michelle and I would drive to the bay and watch as the massive reconstruction of the Bay St. Louis Bridge commenced.

. . . And the animals still lived in the condemned shelter with the high-water line.

One day, Michelle took me to "The Point" in Biloxi. This was a well-known Vietnamese fishing community, and it suffered grave damage. There were few cars and even fewer people. The streets were almost entirely deserted. Some trees had survived, and they were in full bloom. But it was a ghost town. The waterfront was a study in contrasts. For blocks upon blocks, there were lovely green, open spaces. It wasn't until you looked closely that you could see the remains of the foundation slabs of homes. Some of the larger estate homes had miraculously survived Katrina's wrath, the only evidence of damage the blue tarps sealing the roofs. Michelle showed me the neighborhoods where only a few months ago volunteers were furiously trapping stray and abandoned animals. There were no dogs roaming the streets that day.

We headed inland past the casino. The parking lot was full. The building was tall and well-lit in the light of day. Whatever damage it had suffered was gone.

Waveland had begun to show signs of progress. The most noticeable difference was Walmart. By the summer of 2006, the brick-and-mortar store was fully operational; the large white tents no longer needed. The rebuilding and reopening of Walmart was essential to the community. It provided jobs, necessities, and a meeting place for survivors. Its importance could not be diminished.

The animals were doing better, and in large part, it was due to the commitment of Roberta, Chase, William, and Michelle. Roberta and I had entered an unspoken truce, and I treated her with as much respect as I could muster. Anything less would have threatened our fragile relationship. And while people were returning and life was resuming, there were still too many animals. In July that year, we had fifty kittens at the shelter, and there was nowhere to send them. The window of opportunity was closing on receiving shelters willing to take hurricane survivors and their offspring. The novelty had worn off, Katrina fatigue settled in, and the whole country had kittens. And just when Michelle and I thought we had run out of options, my phone would ring with a shelter on the other end of the line. And while we were responsible for so many positive outcomes, I can never, and will never, forget the time we failed.

Dr. Jacquie Broome had reopened her clinic in Gulfport, and her staff was caring for a large litter of Aussie Shepard puppies that had been taken out of Waveland. They cared for those babies for weeks, with ARF and Best Friends footing the bill. A shelter in Maryland had called and wanted puppies. Could we send them? they asked. Michelle and I were thrilled. We made arrangements, got drivers, rented a van, and gave them their health checks. They left on a Friday not long after. The following Tuesday, I received a call from their director. On Monday morning, when the shelter staff arrived, one of the puppies had inexplicably died, and, fearing the worst and having no isolation space for the others, they put the puppies down. They put them all down. The shock and anger I felt was outweighed by my incredible guilt. That I had sent those babies to their deaths. Michelle tried to reason with me as she had used them before while at HSSM. But I couldn't let it go. And while we never sent that shelter another animal, I am haunted by the decision we made that day. I can still see their little faces. I don't know that I'll ever forgive myself.

By late July, many were wondering why I was still working in Mississippi to save animals that we continued to refer to as "Katrina survivors." My refrain became: "I was there because they were." We had found a few small rescue groups in North Carolina and Virginia, and they were in it for the long haul. Dawn Stergin in North Carolina and Lynda Houck in Virginia were able to take a few of our animals and find them good homes. Dawn had adopted out Princess, a Waveland dog, to a woman named Sue and her husband, who only a week prior had lost their dog of sixteen years. Sue's husband was disabled and had come to rely heavily on their dog Gatlin for companionship while Sue was at work. They weren't sure they were ready, but when Dawn introduced them to Princess, they instantly fell for her. A few weeks later, they found out Princess had heartworm, and they were devastated. They thought it was a death sentence, and they didn't know how they'd afford the treatment. Because of the grant money, I was able to call her and tell her we would cover the treatment. She broke down into tears and thanked me over and over again. Princess got her heartworm treated.

In July 2006, I made what would personally be my last trip north to transport animals. Michelle and I rented a passenger van and filled it with twenty-two little souls. After twenty hours with a short stop in Virginia we found ourselves in College Park, Maryland. Both of us exhausted, we couldn't drive any further. There was a Sheraton hotel on our path, so we pulled in. I walked to the reservation desk, looking haggard and no doubt smelling like I'd been in a vehicle with twenty-two animals, and politely asked the woman on duty if they were "dog-friendly." "Oh, yes, we are," she responded politely. I then asked, "Um . . . how many?" With a puzzled look she asked how many we had. Fearing we'd be turned away, I blurted out we were from Mississippi and we were taking them to homes in New England. We had cats too, I told her: five kittens and an adult to be exact. She smiled and called a porter. She then asked if she could come and visit when she took her break.

That night we had thirteen animals in a hotel room in College Park. Daisy, a Waveland dog, headed to a home in Connecticut, had the overstuffed chair and ottoman. Five kittens took over the bathroom, turning the shower curtain into a jungle gym. A litter of six puppies and Luna, an adult cat, had free reign of the room.

By morning, we were well-rested and miraculously had kept the place relatively clean. And when we left the Sheraton at College Park, the staff watched and smiled as we walked through the lobby with our babies in tow.

A year to the day of the thrashing of Hurricane Katrina along the Mississippi Gulf Coast, August 29, 2006, Dr. Jacquie Broome, with the help of Animal Rescue Front, and PAWS Chicago spayed and neutered 276 Hancock County animals. It was a two-day event offered free of charge to Hancock County residents. It was held in the parking lot of the shelter and scheduled for a weekend, and the entire staff were there. Roberta was friendly and engaged with the local folks, helping to comfort the folks who were afraid of the neutering surgeries. Larry and Tori worked hard each day to care for the animals as they awoke from anesthesia. At one point, I sat in the "recovery room" in the lobby of the FEMA trailer and watched as Tori held a small dog that was whimpering as it woke from surgery. Tori was sitting on the floor, her back against the wall, her long blond hair hiding her expression as she looked down at the puppy in her arms. I watched her arms hold the small puppy with such tenderness. The emotion of that moment caught me off guard, and for a minute, I almost forgot where I was and how far we had all come.

On the second day of the event, the Public Works crew next door hosted a barbecue. Barbecue chicken and all the fixings: coleslaw, potato salad, cornbread, and large plastic jugs of sweet tea covered a long table. We laughed and bantered with one another. There's a picture taken that day of Roberta and me on the front stairs of the FEMA trailer. She's leaning on the banister, and my left arm is flung over her shoulders. My smile takes over my face, and she's grinning ever so slightly for the camera. The weekend was an incredible success and brought together those of us who overcame seemingly insurmountable odds since first arriving in Waveland a mere ten months prior.

Weeks before, the local group of business owners who had declined my plea for help that cold winter night had a change of heart. One of them had befriended me and, much to the dismay of some of the others, invited me to stay with her and her husband. Having decided they were leaving the Mississippi Gulf Coast for good, they had recently purchased a house in New Orleans. "The Friends," as the group was called, staffed the phones and scheduled all the surgeries. They helped with the marketing as well. That weekend we ensured that 276 Hancock County animals would not breed again. Not one of those surgeries had a bad outcome. And when PAWS Chicago left to head home, they took every Waveland shelter animal with them. For the first time, perhaps ever, the Waveland Animal Shelter was empty.

"You did some good shit," Roberta said to me late that second night after we had finished cleaning up. And I had to admit: she did some "good shit" too.

Epilogue

By August 2007, a mere two years post-Katrina, the shelter staff of Roberta, Tori, and Larry, responsible for years of terror and suffering, were no longer employed at the Waveland Animal Shelter. A young woman from the north-central United States whose husband had been rebuilding homes on the coast took over shelter operations, and I started a new remote IT position for a San Francisco–based start-up. Animal Rescue Front continued to coordinate transports out of Mississippi and Louisiana, although on a significantly less frequent basis.

The pit bull I had named Petey had a new name and a new life. Now called Wilbur, and living in a family with three small children, his story was featured in a local magazine in Washington State. The woman who drove him all those miles had stayed in touch with me, and when the issue came out, she mailed me a copy. The picture of him sitting on a couch surrounded by the kids brought tears to my eyes.

The Aussie Shepard, who cowered those harrowing first days after I had arrived in Waveland, had been adopted to a middle-aged woman in Washington State as well. She had named her Sarah, and I was told that Sarah slept with her new mom every night in her bed. "It took a few months for her to trust me," her mom said.

Honey Bear was living large with Woody on Cape Cod, and due to the dedication of Buddy's family, his hip and femur had healed better than anyone could have anticipated. Bucks County, Pennsylvania, raised money for the animal shelter in Waveland and it was enough to make it possible for Hancock County to begin plans to build a brand new shelter. The new shelter would be located six miles inland—out of the floodplain.

In 2008 my life was impacted by two major storms: one internal and the other on the Gulf Coast.

In March, my little Macy died of congestive heart failure. For weeks Demi and I were lost without her. Hopelessly, helplessly lost. I could barely catch my breath; my grief was crippling. Demi never left my side, her sadness palpable. The best we could do most days was sit on the couch, where she'd rest her precious head on my thigh.

In the spring of that year, my brother Stephen had been sick with an intestinal condition and, as a result, had lost thirty-five pounds. They couldn't figure out the cause. In May, surgery was scheduled to remove a section of his bowel, but they discovered a stage 3 malignant tumor when they opened him up. The next day my mom was diagnosed with aggressive breast cancer.

Six weeks later, Demi died of a broken heart.

That August, I planned a much-needed vacation in New Orleans. Hurricane Gustav was building in the south Atlantic, and hurricane forecasters predicted it had the potential to be bigger than Katrina. The words "bigger than Katrina" scared the shit out of me but would not prevent me from going through with my plans. If there were going to be another Katrina-like disaster, I'd be there, and I'd be ready.

In the early morning hours of my second day in New Orleans, my phone rang, and it was Chase from Waveland. No longer an animal control officer, he was working for the city's Public Works Department. Chase asked if he could give my number to the new shelter manager. She was very anxious about the threatening storm, and they had no evacuation plans in place.

A few minutes later, my phone rang.

"Hi Chris, this is Linda calling from the Waveland Animal Shelter. Chase gave me your number. This isn't looking good. I have to figure out how to get my animals out of here."

"How many are there?" I asked.

"Eighty-eight," she replied.

I had rented an SUV in anticipation of this potential scenario. It wasn't much, but it was something. A start. Chase had also called In Defense of Animals, and they were rounding up whatever resources they could find. He put us in touch with one another, and I checked out of my guesthouse. This time I headed east on the I-10.

It was August 29, 2008—three years to the day of Katrina.

The governors of Louisiana and Mississippi, once again, declared a state of emergency in their respective states. The declaration kicked off a chain of events that forced the Mississippi Coliseum and Jackson Fairgrounds to open as an evacuation site. Priority would be given to people evacuating with their pets. One thousand cots were quickly assembled in the coliseum and the animal stalls in the large barn-like structure next door was laid with fresh hay. School buses from all over Mississippi congregated in Jackson, where they would soon be assigned destinations in New Orleans, the southern parishes of Louisiana, and the coastal towns in Mississippi. This time they were prepared for the people and the animals.

I posted an online plea for help, and within minutes my phone started ringing. Traci Dawson called and asked what I needed. All I could say was, "Can you come?" She told me she'd get right back to me. In Defense of Animals called, and they were sending a van tricked out with crates for cats and kittens. A large horse trailer was coming for the dogs and puppies. Traci called back and said she and a friend, June Towler, would meet me in Jackson. Linda and I started getting our resources in order. Fortunately, many of the crates we had used after Katrina were found in an outdoor shed. We started to hose them down and get them ready.

By dusk on the evening of August 29, 2008, we were fully prepared to evacuate the Waveland Animal Shelter. With the cargo van filled with the cats and kittens and the horse trailer loaded with dogs and puppies, I asked everyone to hold on for a minute while I walked back inside. I took the same steps I had taken almost three years prior but with one major difference.

This time the cages were empty.

There was not a single sound of suffering or fear. I checked every cage and kennel to make certain we had everyone. They were empty.

Every single one.

Then I walked, alone, to the main light switch, and darkness fell on the Waveland Animal Shelter.

Acknowledgments

A debt of gratitude is owed to so many. *Mississippi Barking* was twelve years in the writing, and was it not for encouraging words along the way; I might have fallen short. To my first reader, Dawn Stergin: you were the one who planted the notion that I could write this book. To the staff at Lemuria Bookstore in Jackson, who cemented my belief that books will save the world. To Pat Hall and Valerie Whalley: you took the manuscript like a football and ran it into the end zone and straight into the arms of the best publisher a writer could hope for: the University Press of Mississippi. I thank you for believing in this project from the moment you were made aware. Huge thanks to my first editor, Abigail Walker, you stoked the flame that had burned out long ago. To Pam Houston, Kelli Bean, "Ms. Imaho," and my women writer friends from the Writing by Writers Lake Tahoe workshop. Your words are liquid gold—write them.

For Michelle Prince, friend, teacher, protector, and partner in crime. Literally. To my Katrina rescue brothers and sisters— heroes, sheroes, all. My life was forever changed to have known you. To Amy E. Hogg, Laurel Ley, and Laura Roggendorf (Bradshaw)and to Best Friends. The best damn animal welfare organization in our country, bar none.

For Carol Guzy, your artistry speaks for itself. Your humanity speaks to us all.

And to the ones we met, the ones we saved, the ones we lost, you're forever in our hearts: your paw prints imprinted on our souls.

To Honey Bear Belle, Phoenix, Trixie, Buddy, Hope, and Red. We loved you. We'll always love you. And to my sister, Althea McLaughlin, the one who broke down the doors that opened the way for thousands to be saved.

Until there are none, save one.

About the Author

Chris McLaughlin is the founder and executive director of the Animal Rescue Front. A graduate of the University of Massachusetts Boston with a BA in earth sciences, she lives in Massachusetts with two cats. This is her first book.